WOMEN: DOWN THROUGH THE AGES

HOW LIES HAVE SHAPED OUR LIVES

by

Jerry Schaefer

authorHOUSE®

AuthorHouse™
1663 Liberty Drive, Suite 200
Bloomington, IN 47403
www.authorhouse.com
Phone: 1-800-839-8640

First published by AuthorHouse 12/5/2007

ISBN: 978-1-4343-5440-2 (sc)

Library of Congress Control Number: 2007909405

Printed in the United States of America
Bloomington, Indiana

This book is printed on acid-free paper.

For my wife, Bea

For those who helped and encouraged me:
Especially Mary Lou and Margo, Jean and Susan,
Meg, Linda, Darlene, Gail and Judy.

And

To Girls and Women everywhere,
who never should have been kicked
out of the Garden,
or blamed for it,
who deserve to simply be.
You are the Garden
the misplaced gardeners.

TABLE OF CONTENTS

INTRODUCTION

The idea for *Woman, DOWN through the Ages* came from Robert McElvaine's book, *Eve's Seed,* Biology, the Sexes, and the Course of History (2001), to whom I'm indebted for important arguments. Women got the shaft in the Garden and it's been downhill ever since. Once men took over the plow, they buried any memory of women's former egalitarian days—enjoyed during the thousands of years as hunter-gatherers--and made sure that women were blamed for anything that went wrong. Many things misfired under the aegis of men's historical run. Women were made to answer for a lot.

The Lie

Central to the story--of Life on earth—is the Lie, because it still dictates how we live our lives today. The Original Lie in the Garden of Eden, that it's women's fault, that Eve tempted Adam--that's the first lie. The second lie follows: that men and women are somehow "defective" or damned—women more so because Eve's to blame. The third, that women are beneath men, to be ruled by men, still haunts us today.

By claiming superiority and taking over the running of the world—basically making war—men had to restrict women to the "fringe" side of life, the home. And, since women are by definition "defective," men wanted to distance themselves as far as possible from this "inferior" sex. They disavowed any semblance of femininity. But, since men do in fact possess feminine qualities, they've had to live a lie for 5000 years, pretending to be what they're not. Since they're less, they act more..

"Civilization" comes out of that lie. It's been war, violence and bloodshed from the start. Today is a replica of Troy. There's always an excuse to be at war: call it Helen, oil, greed or stupidity—it boils down to little boys trying-to-be-tough. While trying to prove, they prove to be trying. Face it: wars are lies, built on lies, sustained on lies, ending in and on lies, in preparation for the next lie. And that's the truth.

Women have been out of the "picture" from the beginning. Without their invaluable input, what could you expect? A world out-of-balance, tottering beneath the weight of endless conflict and warfare—all to profit a bankrupt imagination.

Stop the Blame

The whole catastrophic war-torn planet of today is made possible by fragmentation--someone else is less-than me because of their sex, race, religion, ethnicity, color, speech, dress, class, morals or politics. If all else fails, their shoes. But we all want the basic necessities of life. And there's enough to go around. What's the fuss? The ruling cabals of nations—men, always trying to compete or compensate--say otherwise. So we attack each other, by design. Immigrants, a moving target, are a favorite.

This has been going on for thousands of years, it's all we know. It's in our blood, our being, our language and customs. Some say it's genetic. We're looking at life from Plato's cave, once in a while seeing a reflection of reality, but mostly we're in the dark, being told what we see.

It looks like men own and run the world, but men are owned and run by corporations—those non-human, yet human-made "bodies"—

they are in control. They dictate policy, make life-and-death decisions, and humans are totally out of the picture.

Our "civilization" (not all that civil) is out-of-control, run by men who have no control.

Men Out-of-Balance

Our whole lives are built around pretence and lies. Pretending to girls and women to be something we're not. Pretending to each other that we're "more of what we're supposed to be" (manly) than the other. Men are afraid to be afraid. Scared of fear.

I've been questing for and questioning my "manhood" all my life. Uncomfortable in my skin, living a life of fear, of what? Of being found out? Of not living up to expectations? Whose? In grade school I secretly tried to put weight on my skinny body, using Charles Atlas formulas. No wonder I wanted to be a girl!

We've made token "progress." For a reality check, visit almost any playground-school in the nation. Boys will be preening, sulking, pretending to be on-top-of-things, nervous, as if they've something to hide. They do. Girls will be lively, loquacious and sociable. And, at middle school and beyond, they'll be competing for boys' attention. The "gains" women have made are, sorry, cosmetic.

Women: DOWN

This is a light-hearted (my apologies to women for whom there's nothing "light" about it) attempt to offer a brief sketch of the absurdities that we've put women through, in our attempt to keep a world intact that is riddled with lies. It's too late to blame men, though they seem to take some licks. Its brevity precludes any attempt at scholarliness or thoroughness. I have no idea how to expose the Lie. The difficulty of "cracking" it is as hard as ever. Copernicus was attacked for denying that the sun revolved around the earth. Who's going to risk denying that life revolves around men?

Even now, with glaciers lapping at our shores and winds toppling our dreams, the people who own the world are clueless, being owned by greed. It's beyond incredible. We're still building new freeways, new coal plants, new nuclear plants—it's business as usual because that's *all we know.* Profits and war. That's our life, our livelihood.

The world is a disaster staring us in the face. What do world leaders do? Nothing. They're utterly helpless, hopeless—all they know is the failed civilization that they've built. Their answer won't be to try and cooperate worldwide to salvage our planet. It'll be to wage war and make things worse. That's all *they know.* It's happening in front of our face right now. And without women all-of-a-sudden being admitted into the Holy Sanctum in order to help rescue mankind from this debacle, there seems to be no way out.

Part One

Pre-history to A.D. 500

Chapter 1

Before Men Caught On

In the early days before history got started, men and women treated each other as partners. They didn't have a word for equal, so they used "sequel." And that's what they did; they followed each other around, taking turns. This was known as the "Before-They-Knew-Any-Better" Period which lasted for 200,000 years. This was a good time for women even though they had no appliances.

The period of the Hunter-Gatherers was the best of times (they were always busy finding food and shelter so no one thought of "leisure"). No shopping, no clocks or calendars, they lived in the moment. The moment went on indefinitely, sometimes lasting for hours, days or even weeks. No thought about next week's menu. The women would forage for food, collecting tubers, berries, grasses and nuts. That trait has been passed down to modern women who now collect shoes, an adaptive skill. Meanwhile the men were out hunting rabbits and deer or "lion-kill," an early version of road-kill. Today men use the hunting trait to hunt "prey," so-called because of the prayers they offer up to help them stalk the Female Beast.

Women Lose Their Hair and Gain a Set of Hands

Men and women tended to pair off. Once a woman lost her body-hair, which her baby had clung to, she had to carry him in her arms. Now she needed another set of hands to fend off a hyena if it tried to snatch her baby. Enter the guy with a handy set of hands. They got along reasonably well, and if they didn't, it'd be time for new hands. Sexual relations were somewhat fluid, not to put too fine a point on it. A woman for example might have sex with multiple males as an early form of insurance. Males being males, each one would see his own smug puss in the cute face of the baby. Once they caught on, she'd have to change the policy.

A God for every Purpose

The family units belonged to larger groups that stayed together as they moved from Briarberry Lane to Dogwood Avenue, moving from one camp to another after they ate up all the local goodies. Within this larger group (fifteen to thirty, give or take fifty-eight) they forged social bonds cemented by religious rituals, an early form of glue. They admired animals, especially the ones that could do things they couldn't, which meant quite a few, from running like a cheetah to twisting through the grass like a snake. They didn't yet realize that tigers couldn't think, nor did they imagine they could have "thoughts," not yet having a word for it. We call them "primitive" because they had no sense of fashion, used mostly consonants, spread peanut butter on both sides of the bread, and communicated mostly through movement or dance.

They worshipped the Goddess who allowed new beings to emerge from the stomach of a woman. At different times women themselves were thought to be goddesses. Women neither affirmed nor denied the allegation.

It would take men another 50,000 years to figure out just how women miraculously pulled a perfectly-formed baby out of their mysterious tummies, down through a channel that was more dangerous and mysterious to navigate than 10,000 rivers. Men didn't think they had anything to do with it; farming hadn't been invented yet. To top it off, a woman would then produce milk from her very own nipples, something a man couldn't duplicate no matter how hard he tried, on himself or anybody else. Men spent a lot of time in trees.

Naturally women were revered for their magical powers. Drawings and figurines show women with even-larger breasts than contemporary breast-obsessed men can imagine, as well as prominent genitals and hips as wide as a truck.

Women Deliberately Deliberate

Women had an important role in this early society. Decisions were made by group consensus. Women figured prominently in these deliberations, whether it was deciding when to break camp, how to deal with Thrruw who kept throwing cocoanuts at Tuphia, or what to do about Uvi who complained that Klerty wouldn't put the lid down.

The First People

The Kalahari San are thought to be descendents of the original humans. Their language is !Kung. When Elizabeth Marshall Thomas visited them in 1950, their hunter-gatherer way of life was still intact. Their dwellings were simple grass and brush huts. The men hunted small game, like ostrich, and larger animals such as deer and elephants. When a hunter killed an animal, it belonged to the owner of the arrow that brought it down (even if he were absent). The owner would distribute the cut-up animal, giving parts to the hunting party, then to his wife and her family, then to his parents (and each of them would in turn give portions to their families), then to other members of the tribe till it was all gone.

In *The Old Way* (2006), she pointed out that the women were treated as equal partners. If a wife did not like her husband, she could up and leave and find a new one. Babies and infants were doted on by adults and kids alike. Crying was rare. No one ever struck a child, for any reason. Sounds pretty primitive—they need to be civilized!?

The Shivering Gene

Just when things really started heating up around the old campfire, everyone nice and toasty, wham! Another Ice Age roars into camp, and off they go, icicles dripping down their legs.

There wasn't a lot to do when the Ice Age came. It was, of course, unscheduled; no Weather Channel to turn to for information, so people just couldn't get out of town fast enough. Those that did passed on our shivering gene which heats up our goose bumps. Those that didn't turn around and get turned into blocks of ice managed to find shelter in caves. Lots of down-time ensued as they tried to keep warm while looking at each other in the flickering flames. Long periods of silence eventually led to words. Someone had to break the ice.

How Language Got Started

Sitting around on large ice cubes for chairs can concentrate the mind. It was in these shivering times that men and women started making up words for things. Naturally women took the lead, talking about, what else, men's "things," and what they did with them, and how…especially how! Words were soon flying out willy-nilly, bouncing off the cave walls like an echo chamber. Men took notice and were soon into early locker room banter. Their chairs soon melted under the heat of the conversation.

Let's Dance

More important than language, it was dance that held these early groups together. The British anthropologist Robin Dunbar sees language as subservient to danced rituals (*Grooming, Gossip, and the Evolution of Language*, 1996). It was dance that led them to see beyond their everyday existence, which provided a door to the metaphysical, spiritual realm.

A spurt of creativity was sparked during this Ice Age. Many of the cave paintings date from that time. There are also simple musical instruments carved from bone. Music of course would accompany dance. Barbara Ehrenreich mentions that drawings on the ceiling of a recently discovered cave in England shows "conga lines" of female dancers (*Dancing in the Streets*, Holt, 2006)

Seeding the Future

Once the ice had receded, our ancestors resumed their trek over the land. Women again collected plants and seeds, and, by accident they noticed that dropped seeds would re-grow if left undisturbed: Agriculture. This was initially a positive thing for women. Not only did they pull babies out of their own bodies, now they made things pop up out of the dirt. Men scrambled back up the trees.

The novelty was intriguing: put seeds into the ground, wait a week or so, up comes something green. And tasty. After years of trial and error they realized that it tasted even better and lasted longer if they let it grow for a few months instead of eating it after a few days. More magic from the women who brought you babies. The Earth Goddess gained on the goddities exchange. Fertility goddesses started springing up across the countryside like mushrooms.

Women Replace Sticks With Fingers

It started with wooden sticks and simple hoes, being less wear and tear on the hands and easier to stick into the ground than fingers. This was still mainly women's work though men were welcome to help out. But men couldn't handle it: too much of a come-down from the group camaraderie of the hunt. Men sulked, but what could they say? Women were putting food on the tables, babies in the basket. They still argued over whether she should get bark shoes instead of jute, now that they had fewer bones to pick.

For men it was a disaster. For the first time in pre-history they were out of a job, unemployed. With food popping up out of the ground, men didn't have to go off on hunting expeditions. They were not happy about this drastic change. They waited for the plow. Not knowing what it would bring.

Women Banished from the Field

The "period of the hoe" is usually called horticulture. So many jokes around that word that they couldn't wait for the next phase, agriculture, which came about with the invention of the plow. The plow turned out to be a bad thing for women. It was unwieldy, purposefully heavy, and men made sure that women never got their mitts on it.

The plow allowed men to take over farming, effectively putting women out of "work," real work. They still had to forage for food, skin rabbits, clean and tan the hide, make clothes out of the skin, make baskets, nurse babies, cook, clean the dirt floor and keep the fire going. Part time job at best.

Though men had a job again, they were miserable. Gone was the twenty-five hour workweek. The more successful they were, the harder they had to work. There were more mouths to feed, more land to plow, more things to buy now that people were settled down and specializing in making baskets, bowls, carvings and primitive lingerie. The previous life was an Eden by comparison to the 100-hour-week of sweat and back-breaking labor they now endured. Escape to the trees was no longer possible; they'd been cleared for farming.

CHAPTER 2

SPEAKING OF EDEN

There were always stories going around about why the Sun God went up, then came down, what kind of fermentation the Moon Goddess used to make cheese, how the Forecast God controlled the weather. And why, oh why were they so miserable? What happened to the lush life of the "good ole days?" These things all had to be explained. We now call these stories "myths" to distinguish them from our own fables like Lincoln the LogSpitter, and George Washington who could never lie down.

Shoes and Tractors

One of the myths had to do with Eve's temptation to know her true foot size. If she picked her correct size from the Shoe Tree, she'd be able to put the whole tree into her closet, shoes and all (this version originated in the Philippines). Another up-dated version featured mini-tractors hanging from the branches. The snake offered to give Eve driving lessons (knowledge) if she picked one of the shiny red tractors.

Apples and Ribs

According to McElvaine in *Eve's Seed*, there is a striking similarity between the Adam and Eve myth and the *Epic of Gilgamesh*, a Babylonian tale. Both are allegories about women inventing agriculture. And in both cases, once the knowledge of agriculture is acquired, there goes the neighborhood.

In *Genesis*, chapter two, Eve is formed from Adam's rib, while he sleeps through the whole thing. This is after God has created all the other animals. In chapter three, Eve offers fruit (sex) to Adam. Sex signifies planting seed or farming. This is why they must leave. Eve is trashed, her womb cursed, and out they go, to toil and sweat in the fields. It's Eve's fault. Eve was framed in the garden. Eden was a bad place for women to start out.

The Forgotten Chapter

In the lesser, forgotten story from Chapter 1 of *Genesis,* Adam and Eve are created more or less equal on the 6th day, Eve not taken at all from one of Adam's broken-down ribs. That story didn't play so well, especially with the patriarchs, so they went with Chapter two, Adam on top, Eve due to be ribbed the rest of her days.

The Apocryphal Version

In this story, found amongst the Deadly Sea Scrolls, Adam couldn't reach the apple, so he persuaded Eve to climb on his shoulders and pick one. Thinking it might be poisonous, he then asked Eve to take a bite first. As soon as Eve took a bite, God appeared. Adam pointed his finger at Eve and she took the rap. Women have never since trusted men. With gods like that, can patriarchy be far behind?

Patriarchy

Patriarchy is the calling card of the Old Testament. Instituted by the Assyrians, the Hittites and all the other –ites of the O.T., the Israelites passed it down through history and it's been a huge success, still popular today on the stage of the "civilized" world. It's never played as well among some of the "primitive" peoples who haven't inherited the male obsession with sin and women to blame for it. Patriarchy continues to be an unmitigated disaster for women.

The Israelite people ("people" meant males) had the levirate law which said that if a woman's husband dies, she would go to a close male relative, even if he already had a wife. She was passed around like a fruitcake. Patriarchy means "men own the women." The word "husband" means "master."

Fathers Get Life on a Lease (or leash)

Women were property, pure and simple, part of real estate, good for farming and worker production. Sex belonged in the marriage bed, to replenish the race with men to man the ramparts for battle. If a woman was raped, she had to marry her attacker. A bad thing. If a bride was found to be not-a-virgin, she could be stoned to death. That's ugly. And death to the adulterous wife, but not the husband. Can it get any worse? Yes--daughters could be leased out for a number of years to pay off the father's debt. Everyone seemed to be in debt to each other with daughters going through revolving doors.

Cities Happen

The invention of the plow transformed the lives of everyone. Now it was possible to produce extra food. Surplus food meant trade meant government meant competition meant armies meant war, and war meant women got the shaft. Women and war don't mix. War is bad for women. Period. Cities sprang up. Civilization had arrived with a vengeance. Slavery, classes, greed, oil and Wal-Mart, all of it. And all woman's fault. Whatever bad happens, the finger points to women.

With government came private property. Which had to be protected. With goods being traded, the "middle man" came into being to help with distribution, and hierarchies made sure there were gaps for them to fill. The world had arrived, as we know it.

Men See the Light (at end of tunnel)

Men saw the connection between the furrows of the field and the furrows of women. Seeds were planted in both plots of "land." Women were, after all, dirt. Cheap. A place for seed to be planted. When men had finally figured out that their seed played a part in making babies, it was all over for women. Once men got the notion, they took it to the bank, the seed bank, and they have all the deposits.

Egypt Tries to be Different

There was an exception to the "civilization-is-bad-for-women" idea. Women enjoyed equal rights with men throughout early Egyptian history. A married woman maintained her status as a completely independent legal personality and did not give up her rights to her husband upon marriage. A good thing. She did not need a male cosignatory when she witnessed documents, executed her own last testament, inherited, bought, administered or sold property, freed slaves, adopted children, or sued. A very good thing.

Don't Bring Your Wife to Court

She also testified in courts, even in the highest courts of the land. During the Middle Kingdom a daughter sued her father. A sage of the day advised men against bringing women into court, since they'd (men) probably lose. Men were getting smart, conceding the advantage to women.

A Long Time

Egypt's various dynasties lasted for 3000 years (the USA will be 300 years old in fifty-some years), and in all of that time, women could inherit property, earn the same wages as men, and work at most of the same occupations as men. Daughters shared equally with sons in an inheritance. Unfortunately, Egypt is remembered for Cleopatra's romance with, and subsequent loss in battle to Anthony, not its exemplary treatment of women.

There was no such thing as the "weaker sex." Women as well as men were called up to perform "labor service" for the state, a sort of annual tax that no one liked. They had to work on roads, irrigation canals and other construction projects. This got women out of the house, and kept them away from the shopping malls.

During the time of the Middle Kingdom there were many priestesses, as well as women in professional positions and in politics. Later on, during the New Kingdom, women worked in the perfume industry, some as supervisors. They also had jobs in workshops that made wigs.

Sexual expression was tolerated, even encouraged, and virginity mattered little in arranged marriages. A good thing for women, as they seemed to have a monopoly on it.

Hatshepsut Loses Face

There were some famous women pharaohs. One of them, Hatshepsut ruled Egypt for twenty-one years. She strengthened the position of Egypt by making peace with the tribes of Kush (Nubia) and sending missions to the nations along the East African coast. But upon her death, her stepson chiseled her figure from the wall reliefs with which she had decorated her temples. He failed in his attempt to destroy the memory of Hatshepsut in Egypt. Thothmes III also had difficulty with her name.

Chapter 3

The Classical Period

The Greeks have always had a classy reputation, so we refer to them as Classical, Period. Women refer to them as Geeks; they were not a good omen for women.

Alexander the Pipsqueak

Unfortunately, the women-hating Greeks conquered the women-loving Egyptians when Alexander the Pipsqueak (a.k.a. Great) took over the whole world. After that, a woman living in Egypt either did or didn't have to get a man's permission to go to a movie, depending on whether she was living under Greek or Egyptian customs.

Mother-less Athena

The top Greek god was Zeus, similar to the thunderbolt-throwing god of war, Yahweh. But unlike Yahweh, Zeus had kids, which made things more interesting. Zeus gave birth to Athena by himself, establishing the principle of male dominance and female subordination. Athena always took Zeus' side, and bragged about the fact that she had no mother. Not a good role model for women. In fact, this was the male dream of the early Greeks: to be able to create *themselves*, so they could dispense with women altogether. Women were seen as a testament to the gods' hatred of mankind.

The Olympian gods (they resided on Mount Olympus, home of flowing nectar and beer) and the Athenian State represented order, control, and harmony. Women represented all that is opposed to civilized life, according to Hesiod, a too-well-known early Greek writer. He thought women were evil. They represented passion and instinct, which are not always under control and can be a threat to society, especially a male-dominated one.

Big Plate for Greek Men

To be fair, a Greek man had a lot on his plate. He had to contend with three groups of women: the courtesan, a refined whore; the garden-variety whore, and lastly, his wife, a non-horror. That's a horrible lot.

Neither did the Greeks trust nature. They were always trying to subdue it, control it, dominate it, and of course they identified women with nature. Unpredictable.

Opposites

The Greeks loved opposites, good and bad, cold and hot, etc. and not-etc. The philosophers, having nothing better to do, sat around dreaming up these things. They then applied these to women. Pythagoras, the great mathematician, taught that women were bad, men good. The first "weird" math. Aristotle, the father of philosophy, taught that men were "hot," therefore women were "cold." Since they lacked "heat," a positive quality, women were deformed males, monstrosities. Their menstrual fluid was a weak form of a male's semen. Nothing is known of Aristotle's mother.

Women are Hysterical

Even the Egyptians, a thousand years earlier, talked about women's "problems" and what to do about them. But the Greeks gave us the word "hysteria" which means "from the womb." Hysteria is a disease of the womb, treatable according to Hippocrates (never loath to utter an oath) by exercise and massage. Treatments for hysteria are described from the 4th century B.C. until the American Psychiatric Association dropped the term in 1952, that's A.D.1952.

Humoring the Humors

The Greeks believed that the bodily fluids or humors had to be in proper balance. If any of the fluids were to build up it would be unhealthy. Blocked humors could lead to anxiety, sleeplessness, irritability and nervousness, all symptoms of hysteria. Best to keep things moving, keep her in good humor. Since women had semen-type fluids, just as men did, these fluids needed to be released regularly.

Bring it Down

According to Plato, the famous philosopher who had a habit of hanging out in caves, the problem was the uterus. Disconnected from its moorings, it had wandered up from her belly and was suffocating her. The cure, consistent with Galen, was to "coax the organ back into its normal position in the pelvis and to cause the expulsion of the "excess fluids." This would be a money-maker for doctors in the early 20th century.

Galen Lays Down the Law in the 3rd Century A.D.

Galen was the star Greek doctor of the time. He distilled knowledge from the previous 1000 years and said it's good enough for the next 1700 years. And nobody doubted him. He saw hysteria as a uterine disease caused by sexual deprivation. He prescribed massage therapy which would result in contractions and the release of the trapped, nasty fluids. After this treatment the patient would be relieved of her symptoms. This procedure for hysteria became the therapeutic gospel till the end of the 19th century. Hysteria was not a good word for women's womb.

But it wasn't all bad. About the same time as Galen, Hippolytes, an early bishop of Rome, taught that a woman had to have an orgasm if conception was to take place. This belief lasted, more or less intact into the 18th century, and was a very good thing for women.

The Less-Geeky Greeks

In the Hellenistic Era (the three centuries before Christ), named for the hell-raising god Dionysus, women did better. For one thing the goddess of love, Aphrodite, took over. She was for the first time seen nude. This could be a good or a bad thing, jury's still out looking. Dionysus, the god of wine and partying, who was always raising hell, was also featured on all the billboards of the major camel routes.

There were many mystery rites and hundreds of different local religious cults, many presided over by women. Participants came out of them feeling transformed. It's these kinds of experiences that gave us the word ecstasy (*Dancing in the Streets.*)

The Roman Empire

Now the Romans rolled into town. They took over and ran Venus (Aphrodite re-named) up the flagpole. Bacchus out-swigged Dionysus in a drink-a-thon, so he became the new god of wine. And they set up the *Patriopotestas* (they thought if they put it in Latin, no one would know what it meant) meaning that the legal head of household had absolute power over everybody in the house: slaves, concubines, kids, and wife. This included the right of life and death and the right to sell any and all of them into slavery. This was a bad thing for women, as patriarchic customs were now codified in writing.

Women on the Move

Like the Greeks before them, the Romans didn't consider women as fully human. The "people of Rome" meant the "men of Rome." But, unlike the Greeks, they didn't see women as hostile to civilization. Nor did they have an argument with nature, as did the Greeks. Women moved forward two spaces.

Early Family Values

Once Augustus became emperor, (when Christianity was just getting off the ground) things got bad. He made marriage compulsory. He commissioned the poets to construct a glorious, mythical past that the citizens should try to emulate. He legislated "family values," punishing bachelors, and rewarding women who bore three kids with special privileges. Four was even better, good for an upgrade (a slave woman could become a "freewoman.") Augustus instructed men to enforce marital chastity upon their wives, and he threatened punishment if they failed to prosecute their wives for adultery. Women move back three spaces.

State Takes Over Family Business

With adultery a criminal offense, the state had assumed jurisdiction over the family. The ideal wife was someone who was quiet, submissive and obedient. Where was Dionysus? To make matters worse, Augustus triumphed over Cleopatra in Egypt. This was seen as the triumph of male over female forces. Bad hair day for women.

Women were blamed for the decadence that prevailed in Rome that led to its downfall. They were seen as typifying the immorality of the age and were used as an index of the degeneration that plagued the empire. They needed a savior.

The Early Church

Jesus' teachings were a good thing for women. He treated women as if they were actually people, much to the amazement and consternation of the apostles and the authorities. But it didn't take long for that to change. Once he was gone, the "good ole boys" patriarchal mentality asserted itself.

St. Paul, Unhorsed

St. Paul, the man who was famously knocked off his horse--is he speaking metaphorically? In any case, he, like Aristotle, saw women as "monsters," and thought that they should be veiled because of their imperfections. He turned to the *Torah* of the Old Testament, not the Messiah, to justify the subordination of women. To summarize: God is to man as man is to woman, as master is to slave. Jesus would have rolled over in his grave if he hadn't already rolled out. Women were Jesus' main followers and supporters, and, unlike the flaky Peter, never deserted him.

The Church Fathers

Where were the Church Mothers? Tertullian, one of the early Church Fathers thought that women were agents of the devil. He accused them of bringing death into the world, and he wasn't being ironic. According to him, women led men to sin by being attractive and by dressing in a comely fashion.

Along comes St. Augustine riding in on a 5th century hippo to continue the plummeting stock of women's value. Keep in mind that his mother was constantly on his case to give up his mistress and get married. He agreed, but couldn't keep away from his girl friend, then all-at-once decided to go cold turkey, give up the idea of marriage altogether and be celibate. No more sex. It was a hellish time for him, and he took it out on women. He saw them as temptresses. What are they good for except to be men's helper in bearing children? Sex should be for that and nothing else. If he can't have it, nobody else should either. Spoken just like a man. Good for hippos, bad for women.

In the midst of all this, the Church was getting rather cozy with the Roman Empire. One good outcome for women, contained in the Justinian Code, was the stipulation that the marriage contract was between *consenting individuals.* This gave a measure of autonomy to a woman, released at last from the confines of the antiquated family system where she was basically dry goods, except at certain times of the month.

Women form Coffee Klatches

Clement of Alexandria, another early Church Father, was concerned that women were running around from church to church (often located in homes) to meet with their women friends. This could be dangerous, women talking to each other.

Women were energized by the "Good News." It was still early days, the "lockdown" hadn't happened yet, and women were a vital force in the spread of the new teachings of Jesus. As they met and talked to each other, they inspired each other and found their own sense of self, or realized for the first time that they had one. Who would have thought? The result: they were beginning to be seen as a threat to men because they were rejecting traditional relationships with men in favor of the network of women they had found. Oh, oh, that's not in the script.

SUMMARY

Women lost the equality and comradeship with men that they had enjoyed during the hunter-gatherer period of pre-history, the time before "progress" had begun. Men used the newly-invented plow to bury the memories.

The Old Testament, the book of record for subsequent Western civilization, is a gory book filled with war, killing, a wrathful god, and the subordination of women under patriarchy. Women are not good at war, having an "unfortunate" built-in predilection for life. They were valued simply as property and for their ability to provide further fodder for battle. Soldier factories.

The prophet Jesus had elevated women to an equal stature alongside men, but his example and teachings were quickly twisted by St. Paul and the early Church Fathers, who obviously hated their mothers. Saint Augustine, who couldn't handle the temptations of women, blamed them, not himself. That became the standard position that men would take to the present day. The missionary position.

The Church Fathers blamed Eve, and by extension all women, for her sin in the Garden of Eden. Women accepted the twisted logic of this perverted reasoning which put them beneath men. Their subsequent second-class citizenship is blamed on this original scene wherein Eve was framed.

Quiz # 1 Pre-History to Post-History

1. When a man saw a baby being born his first thought was:
    a. Damn why didn't I think of that?
    b. If she does that again, I'm outta here.
    c. I just wish I had something to do with it.

2. Draw some early figurines, using a truck as a scale.

3. Talking began when:
    a. Women let their hair down (assuming it was ever up)
    b. Ice began to melt between their legs
    c. Men saw how words could further their endeavor (explain endeavor)

4. Women invented agriculture to:
    a. show how unemployment worked
    b. extend their field of fertility
    c. keep the guys at home

5. Why didn't Adam and Eve try to sneak back into Eden after dark?

6. How many shoes did Eve pick before she found her size? How big was her closet?

7. Do you think Eve liked Adam? Maybe fonder of the snake?

8. Was Adam sorry he ever wanted a partner? Would he have been better off with one of the other animals? Who or which?

9. Did God forget what he wrote in Chapter 1 by the time he got to Chapter 2? Did he think we wouldn't notice?

10. During the Ice Age:
    a. men discovered the locker room
    b. words were used to melt ice, providing a warming trend
    c. women named men's parts first and men didn't even try

Part Two

The Middle Ages: A.D. 500 to 1350

Chapter 4

Germanic Tribes Come to Rome to Shop (Then Decide to Stay)

Hordes of Germanic Shoppers, called barbarians since many of them were free-lance barbers, invaded Rome in the 5th century (May 23, A.D. 410 at 6:01 PM) just when the stores were closing their doors. Imagine, coming as far as they did, then told to come back the next morning! They went on a rampage, broke into the stores and shopped all night, filling their sacks to the brim. This came to be known as "The Sacking of Rome."

Nothing much was left of Rome after this "sacking," so the Romans, themselves thoroughly sacked due to debauchery and generally high living, which they blamed on women, simply threw in the towel. The mighty Roman Empire was brought down in a fire sale—the first fire sale in history--by hordes of shoppers.

More Sacking and Shopping

The invading Germanic Tribes intermarried with the Romans, both sides thinking they were marrying "down." And as Rome re-stocked its shelves, it got sacked again and again as other Vandals and Visiting Goths heard about the bargains to be had. The period from the 5th to the 11th century was a sort of rough-and-tumble frontier time for Western Europe. Women, who seem to thrive in situations of fluidity and chaos before male "order" sets in and they're ordered around, played a vital role in laying the foundations of our modern society.

Monasticism

Chaos followed the collapse of the Roman Empire's shopping malls, and in the 6th and 7th century, monks and nuns tried to civilize these wild-eyed shoppers and teach them to buy prayers and indulgences (on the Futures Market).

Once the Germanic kingdoms were in place, the nuns and monks went chasing after them to convert them to Christianity. They set up monasteries in the wilderness, and abbesses, female abbots, were often in charge of these warehouses of prayer.

Nuns and Monks Set up House

The most popular house for women in the seventh century was the double monastery—one side for women, the other side for the men folk--in which religious men and women observed the same rules and obeyed a common superior, usually a woman. The Christian doctrine that men and women are spiritually equal made it okay for men to be ruled by a woman, for now.

Watch Those Hands

The early Germanic law codes regarded women as property belonging to the family. Nothing new. The marriageable girl went to the highest bidder. But they did believe in protecting the modesty of women or their virtue, whichever came first. If a man pressed the hand of a woman, he paid a fine of fifteen *solidi* (about the price of a hen), above the elbow would cost him thirty-five *solidi* (about the price of an egg-laying hen—jumbo size if above the elbow but below the 3rd vertebra).

Meanwhile, over in France, the Franks were the first tribe to embrace orthodox Christianity even though the first son of king Clovis and his wife Clothilde died upon being baptized. The king was so outraged when the monk excitedly explained the baby would go straight to heaven that he almost dispatched the monk directly there. Once converted, the families had their own version of Christianity, including polygamy, incest, and a most bizarre custom of the battlefield. Widows, who were seized on the battlefield where their dead husbands lay, had to marry the murderers. This renovated version of Christianity was bad for women.

Slaves Move Up

Some Frankish slaves and peasant women used their "charms" to advance themselves. The slave Fredegonda became queen when King Chilperic married her after he murdered his Visigoth wife in the 6th century. Bathilda, another slave, became queen as the wife of Clovis II. Not forgetting her origins, she tried to put a stop to the slave trade, not wanting to be replaced by a younger slave.

Monasteries Compete with Marriage Bed

The English chronicler Bede suggests that a whole generation of women from the royal Anglo-Saxon families chose the celibate life of the convent over marriage. Women fled to the cloister before and after marriage to get away from the ownership society of men. Men probably thought that women simply preferred deprivation and that it had nothing to do with them.

The Carolingian Age: A.D. 700 to 900—Women Move Down.

After centuries of Vandals running rampant over ramparts, of Ostrogoths arguing with Visigoths over who was more "goth," of Picts and Scots competing with Huns over who's best at beheading and raping, finally an emperor took over and introduced some order into the chaos: Charlemagne, for whom the Carolingian period is named.

Reforms Bad for Women

Church and state, now united, tried to control polygamy, end the practice of concubines for the clergy, and stop divorce. Naturally women were to blame for all of the above. These attempts revived and reinforced misogynistic ideas. Ideological attacks on women rose sharply, and the first accusations of witchcraft occurred at this time, with the execution of Gerberga, a nun. This was before brooms so we're not sure what her offense was.

Womanish Monks who can Read

The Emperor Charlemagne forbade nuns from educating boys in their convents He stated that the "weakness of her sex and the instability of her mind" would prevent them from exercising leadership over men. Since noble ladies could still be raised and educated in convents, and these were the only learning places in town, it meant that for a few hundred years it was common for a female, with an "unstable mind" (yet educated), to be wed to an illiterate husband. Monks of course continued their studies, and the knightly class referred to them as "womanish," because they could read.

Ninth-Century Changes—Women Move Up

Secular women of the 9th century were now able to own some property and the Germanic custom of bride purchase was out of fashion. Instead, the groom now gave his bride a piece of property, increasing her independence after marriage. They could also inherit property, a practice previously forbidden.

Queens Put to Work

The wives of kings were now expected to do more than sit around on their throne knitting socks. They had the duty of running the royal estates, as well as taking care of the finances and domestic affairs of the realm. The king had more important matters, like setting up the Knights of the Royal Garter and investigating hem lengths.

The Carolingians started the practice of crowned women participating in the royal rule.

Instead of the "king's wife," she was now the "Queen." And she and the other women of the nobility played chess, on and off the board.

Marriage Cannot be Dissolved

Even wives gained a bit. Marital indissolubility, formerly a church matter, now was part of secular legislation. Grounds for repudiation were limited to adultery. Even childlessness, the default fault of the woman, wasn't sufficient reason to dump her. This wouldn't last.

Women Heating Up

When King Lothar II attempted to repudiate his wife Tetberga , so that he could marry his mistress Waldrada, Tetberga successfully underwent the ordeal of boiling water—designed to bubble out the truth—and thereby negated the charges of adultery and incest. The water was then raised ten degrees for incest. The marriage still wouldn't dissolve.

The Pollution Solution to Large Families

Family size among the lower classes tended to be small, as they attempted to match the number of children with their resources. Women were willing to risk seven years of penance, which was the penalty for a woman who killed an unborn child by "magical practice, by drink or by any art." Birth control was prohibited as being against nature, and sexual relations were for the sole purpose of baby-making. Theodulf, a churchman called it "pollution," when a man lies with a woman in an unnatural fashion, not intending childbirth.

As the control of the Church and State came to be vested in the hands of men in this time of empire, women's activities were restricted to the home and the cloister. The reforms elevated the monogamous family to be the basic economic unit, and they helped to strengthen class divisions among the propertied caste.

Still, within the family, women's rights were made stronger by the indissolubility factor. The husband could no longer dissolve his wife in solvent just to get rid of her. He had to have a reasonable solvent.

The First Feudal Age: Tenth and Eleventh Centuries

When the Carolingian empire collapsed, due to improper scaffolding and a shortage of rebar, the family emerged from the rubble as a very effective stabilizing agent, better than putty. And women for the next two centuries played a powerful part.

This was the age of Feudalism, when things were rather futile for the serfs because the serfs *belonged* to the land that they worked. When the land was transferred from one owner to another, the serfs were part of the deal. Under this system, "vassals" oversaw land that belonged to lords. Instead of rent, the serfs paid with crops and military service.

Women's Work Valued (in death)

Woman workers were more valued than men under feudalism. The *wergeld*, the money paid in case of death, was *twice as much for women as it was for men*. On the other hand, the lord's "right of the first night," his privilege of sleeping with the bride of his serfs on their wedding night, was recognized by law and custom well into the 19th century. Today it's more of a custom.

Women on Top

Land was the sole source of power, and women had secured the right to own and inherit it. For two hundred years they played a substantial role as mistresses of landed property and castles with the attendant rights of justice and military command. They were also proprietors of churches and participated in both secular and ecclesiastical assemblies. Good time for women, if you weren't a serf.

Women on the Bottom

But the biggest long-term contribution in this era lay in the anonymous work of peasant agriculture. Two breakthroughs led to surplus production: crop rotation, and the use of nonhuman sources of energy—the horse and mule, the water mill, and later the windmill. Peasant women, who worked the fields just as much as the men, deserve credit for Europe's agricultural revolution. Wives commonly received farm implements and tools for cloth production as wedding gifts. Fortunately, gift-wrapping hadn't started yet.

Women in the Middle

In northern Italy, enterprising women followed lucrative crafts: wool-working, textiles, felt-making and hat manufacture—which became regular exports. Throughout Europe, family workshops in emerging towns produced a wide range of products for trade. Women worked as brewers, glassmakers, and textile workers, or in sales as fishwives. They were associates of their husband in the heavier industries of coopering (barrels of fun), smithing (each took out a policy on the other first), tanning, and salt-panning. And of course garters for the future Order of the Garter.

Women Off to War

Noble ladies held the castles when lords fought in the field, but some women left to fight. When the Normans entered the Mediterranean area and carved out a kingdom in Sicily and southern Italy, women fought along with men. Gaita accompanied her husband on horseback, helmeted and armored. If any of her Norman knights got scared, she rallied them back into the line of battle. And they enjoyed seeing her scarves flying in the wind.

Women Off to Peace

Women have always been peacemakers. A good example was Matilda, sister of Otto II of Germany, Abbess of Quedlinburg. When her brother was busy with the government in Italy, she ruled in his place, even presiding over church councils. She was able to bring peace to Germany, something men knew little about. Women did it all during this period: military leaders, judges, and controllers of property. What would they do next?

The First Pornocracy in Italy: Ruling from the Couch

Some of these independent and powerful women shocked the monkish chronicler, Liutprand of Cremona. He thought the world was in the grip of a horrible "pornocracy," government by prostitutes.

If a woman beckoned from her perfumed couch, Liutprand reasoned, no man could help but do her bidding. According to him, Ermengarde, the daughter of the Marquess of Tuscany, held the highest authority in all of Italy. Her power, he said, came from the "carnal commerce" that she carried on with everyone, prince and commoner alike. An equal opportunity purveyor.

Even the papacy was involved. The pope was under the thumb of Lady Theodora, primarily, and then her daughter Marozia. Mistress to one pope, and mother of another pope, Marozia gained power through her marriage to the king of northern Italy.

Good or Bad?

Though some chroniclers of the time saw women's influence as evil, bishops, eager to reform and put in place good government, relied on the ladies who controlled appointments to local churches. They asked them for their help in restoring out-of-whack parishes and monasteries going to seed.

Islam: Woe to Woman

Islam, like Judaism, held woman to be decidedly inferior creatures. They were the property of men, who could have up to four pieces of baggage. The Koran refers to women as fields to be planted, and of course, crop rotation is easier to practice with multiple fields. Ghazali, an 11th century Muslim theologian, said that all the trials, misfortunes, and woes which men suffer from come from women.

CHAPTER 5

GREGORIAN CHANT DOOMS WOMEN

Once Gregorian Chant was introduced by Pope Gregory (1073-1085), it was all over for women. Up to now, women and men had similar opportunities and there was nothing unusual about women in authoritative positions. But after the Norman Conquest, things were different. Women were simply not as good at the musical rage of the time, the so-called Gregorian Chant. They had to sit way in the back, sometimes outside the church, and nobody could hear them.

Beginning of the End: Sex Roles

By the 12th century, new attitudes began to take over and women had to take cover. Churchmen began to talk about "sex roles" and the different capacities of men and women. Women always come up short when capacities are involved. They're not good at visualizing quarts and football fields.

Darned Socks Anyway

A man could easily be damned for all eternity if he darned his socks—because that was supposed to be women's work. Darned if he did, and damned too. The Church restricted the wide variety of roles that women had played in the previous 10th and 11th centuries.

Clerical Celibacy

There was now an active campaign against clerical marriage and the rights of priest's wives. There had always been complaints about the wives spending too much on wine and not producing enough altar boys, but now with gender differences in the wind, the clamor picked up steam. Pope Gregory VII vowed to enforce clerical celibacy. He offered priests free chastity belts for their wives. He'd keep one key for security.

Down with the Laity

Popes went all-out to get rid of lay influence, from the laity. They were called the laity because they didn't stand up to the pope. The idea was to get rid of the secular role altogether, and make the religious part all-powerful since the pope was in charge of that branch of the world. If you didn't obey him, he'd cast a spell on you, and you'd have to purchase a special indulgence from Dante on the futures market, to move up a level. The goal: to establish a hierarchical church under the absolute control of the papacy. Which is what they did, and it worked until they ran out of indulgences.

Out with the Doubles

As part of the Gregorian reforms, which he named after himself, Pope Gregory ordered the dissolution of the double monasteries—these, ruled by women, further weakened their crumbling place in the church hierarchy. Monasteries, no longer the centers of learning, were replaced by cathedral schools and universities, under the thumbprint of the church. They trained clerks for the priesthood and women were excluded. In the following decades of the 12th century, secular institutions followed the church's lead and restricted women's access. This was a bad trend for women.

Dancing in Church

According to Ehrenreich (*Dancing in the Streets*), dancing in churches was quite common in the late Middle Ages. Priests danced, women danced, as well as the congregation. Despite efforts by the hierarchy, Christianity, to an extent, remained a danced religion (when exported to Africa in modern times, the natives referred to it as "the religion that forbids dancing). The Lateran Council of 1215 instituted a new means of control: each person needed to make an annual "confession." One of the sins: dancing.

Though it was "immoderate" or "lascivious" dancing that the Church railed against, it was dancing within churches, a traditional church custom, that they wanted to root out. Time for some pews.

Love and the Medieval Lady

Medieval courtly love allowed for the expression of sexual love by aristocratic women. It was a relationship of mutuality, and included the idea of homage and freedom for her. Symbols on the knights' shields illustrated the knight in a ritual attitude of commendation, kneeling before his lady with his hands folded between hers. Homage signified service, not domination, a welcome change.

This relationship between knight and lady was at odds with the patriarchal idea of female chastity, meaning the woman's strict bondage to the marriage bed of the beloved. To get around that, the courtly love crowd simply detached "love" from marriage. The Countess of Champagne ruled that, "love can exert no power between husband and wife." And that was that.

Adultery for Women

While courtly love might have satisfied the erotic needs of men, it also helped to refine their attitude towards women. And it gave lovers to women who were their peers, not their masters. For the first time, adultery was justified for women, something men took for granted in patriarchal society.

Love without Sex

Christianity had elevated "love" by purging it of sexuality. Sex was permitted in marriage out of necessity and directed toward procreation. Love, defined as "passion for the good" by Thomas Aquinas, properly directs itself toward God. Thomas, who had no doubts regarding women's abject status, never met one that he couldn't categorize.

Lancelot the Rebel

Lancelot defied Christian teaching by reattaching love to sex. He cared not a whit for "mere sexuality," but experienced love as a devout vocation, as a passion. In Christian Europe, "passion" had a very positive meaning that it lacked in classical times. In the throes of their "passion," courtly lovers, like religious people, sought a higher emotional state, ecstasy, and this demanded heroic discipline. Courtly love wasn't for weaklings.

The Church, for its part, was thrilled with the idea of courtly love's "passion" being fueled by the "exaltation of love." They assumed such love could only be aimed toward God, unaware of the many moving targets.

Who Cares About Legitimacy?

This courtly love "blip" on the patriarchal radar screen was allowed to go on because of property, power, and the role of illegitimacy. Inheritance by women suited the needs of the great landholding families, and this gave some women a strong hand in marital affairs. The husband's primary aim was to get and maintain a fief, a piece of land, and this required his wife's support, maybe even her inheritance. A baron was more concerned about a secure tenure than a legitimate son.

Women Give Voice

Women gave poetic voice and status to female sexual love and medieval Europe accepted it. Eleanor of Aquitaine was one of the pop-stars of courtly love, and she transmitted the fluttering-eyelid gene to her daughter and granddaughter. It was Eleanor who brought courtly love to England, and she and the circles she moved in dispersed it to European nobility. She even tried to export it to America, but they had no courts, nor was it "discovered" yet.

Abelard Cut Down to Size

Abelard was the head philosopher at the University in Paris in the 12th century. He took up lodging at the home of the brilliant Eloise's uncle so that he could tutor her. His tutoring turned to seduction, just as he had planned, and they fell passionately in love. She was willing to be his mistress or whore, but he insisted they marry. She consented though it would end up ruining her life.When their child Astrolabius was born, he moved back to Paris, leaving her with baby Astrolabius. The uncle of Eloise then had Abelard castrated by some thugs. He didn't approve of "Astrolabius".

That cooled Abelard's ardor considerably and he joined a monastery. He convinced Eloise to join a nunnery against her own wishes. He didn't want her to have a life of her own. When the owners of Eloise's nunnery re-possessed it, Abelard bequeathed to her the monastery that he was in charge of—he wanted to get away from the monks under his supervision after they tried to poison him.

Changes in 12th Century Dowry and Marriage

During the previous era, women had increased their savings, continued to own property, and they still received wedding gifts from their husbands, often in cash. They could buy and sell property and were allowed to designate their own heirs. But things were about to change.

No Dowry, No Marriage

After 1140, especially among affluent families, new civil statutes brought back the "Roman dowry," a gift to the groom from the wife's family, and outlawed other gifts to her. To justify the Roman dowry, they simply referred to Aristotle's idea that men are active, women are passive. Therefore the dowry passed through the passive woman to her husband who had his active hands outstretched. Women passively opposed this and no one noticed.

Gratian, who taught at the University of Bologna and trained the lawyers who practiced in towns throughout Italy, put it simply: no dowry, no marriage. Legally the dowry belonged to the wife but she didn't have access to it unless her husband died or she bequeathed it to her children. As more and more capital was transferred from one family to another via the dowry, a woman's wishes in her choice of marriage partner mattered little because so much rode on this transfer of funds. This was not good for women, as she was being used as an off-shore bank.

Things worsened in the late 14th century as the Black Plague wiped out much of the population. Dowries got bigger and bigger and there were far fewer marriages. Unmarried women became a substantial group for the first time in Europe. The age of the bride and groom kept widening with the girls marrying at an ever-younger age. Soon the bride's first task was to begin construction of a casket for her erstwhile husband.

Origin of Old Maids

Poor families contracted their daughters into domestic service to earn a dowry. Urban families, if they had the money, would place their daughters in a convent where the dowry was smaller. Among the poorer classes, women postponed marriage or didn't marry at all. The tendency to associate "maids" (unmarried girls) with "domestic servants" made the two terms almost synonymous.

Mother Goose and Upward Mobility

Dick Whittington of Mother Goose ran away to London-town with his cat and became Lord Mayor. That was possible for a man, but the only mobility open to girls was a suitable match which might even take her in the wrong direction. Up or down, her family taught her the virtues of passivity and obedience in order to win the wedding cake.

There Goes the Inheritance—Royal Dowries into the Pool

With state-building a primary concern in England, queens who often brought great estates and titles into the marriage, now lost authority over their own holdings. They were simply put into the royal "kitty," pooled with everything else. Royal women's influence now depended on her intimacy with the king. That meant that a royal mistress had the same opportunity as the queen. A definite downturn on the queen market.

Prostituting for Dowries

The dowry situation got even more dower. Preachers railed against poor urban parents for prostituting their daughters in order to earn a dowry. On the other hand some women did well in this lucrative profession and were able to retire by marrying. Others ended their careers with the Repentant Sisters of Saint Mary Magdalene. They had to wear girdles made of rosary beads.

Another avenue to get a dowry was to contract young girls to affluent households. Girls as young as eight (*fantine*) did this in Florence. The master owed them only clothes, sheets and daily food because he agreed to provide them with a small dowry at sixteen-years-of-age. Usually the master's intentions were less than honorable and these girls would be well versed in the marriage bed before they earned the right to their own.

Women Start and/or Join Religious Groups

Some women opted out altogether and started informal religious groups like the Beghards, dedicated to reforming society. But the church hierarchy soon clamped down on these "makeshift" orders, declaring that "strict enclosure" was the only way they could channel their religious practices. The Church wanted them behind walls, their walls.

Women resented enclosure. Many had formed bonds and desired to remain as a group "in the world" and continue to follow Christ in their own fashion. As a result, they joined heretical groups that offered greater participation and equality to women. The Albigensians made many converts among women, and the Hussites of Bohemia numbered women among their most dedicated followers and noblewomen among their patrons. These heretical sects were wiped out by the Church, their members burned.

Heretical Behavior

Beatrice de Planissoles of Montaillou, was imprisoned as a heretic in 1322, not for religious beliefs but because she admitted to various sexual liaisons in her village, admitted to having her four well-loved daughters tutored so they could learn to read and write, and she formed close bonds with the peasant women in her community regardless of her noble name and status. Guilty on all counts.

In the Bedroom

As long as we're here, sex was considered by the church to be for procreation only, not pleasure, an idea that the church has always cherished. Accordingly, in England in the 12th and 13th centuries the church made it illegal to have sex on Sundays, Wednesdays, and Fridays, as well as forty days before Easter and Christmas (they wanted to make it four-hundred days but cooler heads prevailed).

After all, they reasoned, it was women and her wicked ways that were to blame for man falling from grace. Some Christian authorities in the Middle Ages referred to women's genitalia as the "yawning mouth of hell."

The Order of the Garter

But some were willing to defend that dangerous place. England's highest order of knights, founded by Edward III in the 14th century, was called the Knights of the Garter. Their famous motto was: "*Honi soit qui mal y pense*"—'Shame on you if you see evil in this', or the contemporary translation: "Honey, it's okay no matter what they say." "This" (or "it") refers to the vagina, according to the medieval scholar Belvali. The Order of the Garter was good for women. Later garters were questionable.

Note: if you want to see for yourself, visit St. George's Chapel at Windsor, the spiritual home of the Order of the Garter. The chapel is covered with symbols representing female genitalia. Don't ask the guide to point them out.

Hysteria

In medieval texts, it's not called "hysteria." It's the "disease of the womb." But they used Plato's account of the uterus wandering around the body, turning up in all the wrong places. It was particularly bad when it crawled up into the windpipe and caused difficult breathing and strangulation. The panting and shortness of breath associated with the disease was called "the suffocation of the mother." They could make up anything. The venomous and corrupt uterine humors needed to be purged, just as men needed to be purged of their own humorous seed. Though men's humors, being opposite, were not corrupt and vile. Men's sense of humor was bad for women.

Treating the Disease

Since sexual deprivation was believed to be the cause of this disease, marriage was prescribed (or horseback riding). For widows and nuns, the "balance of humors" would have to be addressed in other ways. No easy solutions there.

CHAPTER 6

GENDER INTRODUCED IN THE 13TH

In the 12th century the Scholastics, Catholic philosophers, had toyed with polar schemes, putting women down, claiming men were up. But in the 13th century, Thomas Aquinas used Aristotle's inane notions about the "natural order." He claimed that they were ordained by God himself. In his famous *Summa Theologica*, a best-seller in all the local pubs, since it provided a justification for the fermenting of beer as part of god's plan, Aquinas defined woman as the opposite of man. That meant she was passive, material (not spiritual), and deprived of the tendency toward perfection. The "natural order" is not favorable for women, being too artificial.

Let's play opposites

This scheme was so simple it immediately became a hit. Anybody could play the game: find an opposite quality to that of a man and assign it to a woman. Laypeople, even the illiterate, could grasp polarities and use them as unquestioned assumptions. Men are intelligent, women are stupid; men have pipes, women lack proper plumbing. Best of all, they were stamped "credible" by theologians. Incredibly bad for women.

Women Enjoy Sex More

What? How can that be? Albertus Magnus, another great 13th century theologian, reversed traditional thinking when he argued that women enjoy sexual intercourse more than men (*Eve's Seed*, McElvaine, McGraw-Hill, 2001). But, he added, that's because of women's imperfection. Since they're imperfect, they desire union with the "perfect male" more than he does with the "imperfect female." Continuing his distorted logic, he echoed Aristotle by saying that women are defective and misbegotten and that man is "the beginning and end of woman." What did the not-so-great theologians say?

It's no wonder that virginity was highly revered in the Middle Ages. Women liked it because it gave them more independence. Nobody owned them except Christ, and he was gone.

Women as a "Notion"

Thus it was that "gender" was born. It was based on "notions" rather than more rigorous "ideas," (like truth or beauty) which Medieval theologians subjected to a barrage of laser-like, penetrating review that might require thousands of hours of deep thought and years of discourse. By contrast, this new definition of woman passed on an inherited system of notions that remained unexamined. Conceived at church schools, ideas that were unthinkable in earlier centuries went unchallenged in the 13th century. Women, banished from these places, had no idea what they were concocting till it was too late. As in subsequent decisions regarding women, they would be informed later.

This "polar framework" remained fixed, and new comparisons could be dreamed up to fit new circumstances. Men are on-the-move, women are back-sliding. Men have their head in the sun, women don't take a shine to it. And on and on. A philosophical foundation was being laid for the man-centered world.

These polarities were now part of the mental makeup of learned authorities and could be used to justify excluding women from whatever came up. And sometimes, just for fun, they'd make things up just to exclude women, like men fly airplanes, women broomsticks. Polarities were polarizing, which was the whole idea.

Polar Medicine

After the Black Plague (1348-1350) which killed about half of the population of Europe, university-trained physicians prescribed cures according to their own notions of men's and women's polar natures. Not the best medicine for women: if something worked for men, it probably wouldn't for women.

Women's Minds Undermined

The accepted beliefs of the time: that women are born inferior, have a weaker mind and intellect, are more subject to emotions and sexual temptations than men, and that they need to be ruled by men—all of these had a devastating effect on women's minds. These beliefs had been handed down for centuries and women themselves had come to believe and accept them.

Can Women Think?

For example, when an exceptional woman came along and questioned these assumptions, which meant that she was *thinking on her own*, she had to spend a great deal of time and energy apologizing for the very fact that she was in fact *thinking*. She had to prep her readers and listeners to get through the firewall that patriarchal thinking had installed, so they could listen to her words and not think there was a male ventriloquist using her mouth.

If a woman asserted her right to speak, in effect claiming that she could be the author of her own voice and thoughts, she was a self-defined freak. Where did she get the authority to speak? (People were still asking this same question in 19th century America of the Grimke sisters who spoke against slavery)

Over a period of 900 years, up to the 17th century, a woman's right to think and write remained controversial and disputed. To get around this, women writers claimed they were writing "from the heart" (not the brain), or that their discourses were merely "rearranged ideas" (not creative thoughts) or that their ideas were not their own but inspirations from God. They were merely "trumpets of God."

Hildegard of Bingen: Ignorant but Learned

Hildegard, one of the most learned women of the 12th century, referred to herself as "*ignota*," an ignorant woman. Her visions, which began at the age of five, were legitimated by the Church, strangely enough, and she had the ear of both the pope and the Holy Roman Emperor. But even she accepted that women are weaker and therefore destined to be subordinate to man.

Upgrade for Women

Hildegard, "God's little trumpet" as she referred to herself, scored two for women's position. First, she declared that: (1) Only if women and men love each other in marriage will their offspring turn out right. If either partner does not love the other, the child will turn out to be a girl or an embittered boy. Yikes! This meant that women played a part in the outcome; her feelings and attitudes were important.

(2) Hildegard removed the blame for Original Sin from Eve (and women). She said the Fall was preordained by the bodily weakness built into Eve by the creator. An upgrade predicated on a downgrade.

Early Zen

Hildegard's visions fuse the male and female elements, the physical and the spiritual, and she avoids any concept of hierarchy in favor of wholeness, roundedness (she liked curves, circles and waves) and integration. Hildegard was good for women, ahead of the curve.

Women Become a Category

With the church and state becoming more bureaucratic, causal notions in the hands of lawyers became legal precedents. Gratian, who codified Ecclesiastical Law into Canon Law in A.D. 1150, wrote about woman's "incapacity." He offered this as rationale against woman's exercise of positive legal rights. He was speaking of women as a whole, not just one particular woman who, for some reason or other, might find herself "incapacitated." Europeans now began to speak and think of "woman" as a category rather than of a particular woman that they might know. Bad enough being genderized, categorized was even worse.

This tendency became important in justifying women's place in Christian society. It helped define their roles, responsibilities and rights. With this new notion of gender, women now found themselves being directed, rather than directing activities as they had done in the past. They were being scripted in a bad play.

Gender: Ordained by God

Gender expectations came to be the organizing principle of society. "Womanly" conduct was ordained by God and sanctioned by earthly institutions. Since it was part of the "natural order," it couldn't easily be changed. This was brought out in the world of fantasy in Carnival, when women dressed in men's clothes and walked boldly in the streets. This was a ritual enactment of the absurdity of women failing to uphold their ordained roles, even while women mocked those roles.

Thus the system of gender had become conventional wisdom and came to be policed by the people themselves. It's bad to be policed when you don't know you're the policewoman.

What's the Answer?

In economic hard times, with difficulties stemming from chronic warfare and concern over plague epidemics, people sought answers. Absurd Scholastic notions about gender and women gained credibility. And they were applied to the world of work.

For example, a master glass cutter's widow who kept working at the craft after her husband's death could not take on an apprentice. The men of the guild didn't believe that a woman could master it well enough to teach a child, since the craft is a delicate one. As a medieval provost explained, men are "right" or dexterous in the lucrative trade of glass-cutting; women are "left" or clumsy. This belief was justification for eliminating them from positions of authority within the guild.

Yet women practiced the even more dexterous work of lace-making. Even the most exquisite, expansive, and fiercely difficult lace-making could be fit-in around household tasks and child-rearing, so the idea of women's clumsiness didn't need to be applied. The "traditional" division of labor recognized today had taken root, and notions of gender came up as needed to sustain it. The division of labor was bad for women. It even caused divisions amongst women themselves, always a welcome side effect for those in charge of enforcement.

SUMMARY

Women began this period ruling over men in monasteries, the centers of learning. By the end of it they couldn't get in the door. Out of these men-only institutions were hatched the ludicrous ideas about women's "nature" being so different from men's that they could no longer teach men, much less rule over them. The polarities followed: men are smart, women are dumb. After women were genderized—compared unfavorably with men—they were categorized. They were expected to dress, act and live as a distinct category, no exceptions.

The Roman dowry came back, forcing families to prostitute their daughters in order to gain the price of marriage. Women's ability *to think* comes into question, as it will for centuries to come. How can she think if she has no mind? Men have minds, women have purses.

Quiz #2

1. Why didn't the Roman Malls stay open longer? If the Barbarians were given discount coupons, would Rome still rule?

2. How many *solidi* would it cost to touch a girl above the knee but below the elbow?

3. Charlemagne forbade nuns from educating boys because:
    a. the nuns' sex had been weakened
    b. nuns had never properly been stabilized and tottered easily
    c. nuns had no sense of their humors.

4. What was the maximum temperature to dissolve a marriage?

5. The Order of the Garter was set up to:
    a. regulate garter length
    b. ensure that attention was directed below the garter
    c. ensure that garters were ordered properly, by size, etc.
    d. assure women that all was right with the world

6. The Church wanted to restrict women to:
    a. darning socks
    b. making roles
    c. making altar boys

7. The problem with chastity belts was:
    a. the lock could rust…ouch
    b. the husband might forget…oops
    c. the key might be on E-bay…oh, oh

8. The Natural Order was:
    a. monks led by Thomas Aquinas
    b. the way things are ordered by the church, naturally
    c. an Order of nuns who celebrated nature and dressed naturally

9. Gender was Thomas Aquinas' gift to women. T/F

10. Women were not able to teach glass-cutting to a child because:
    a. the child would be left thinking he/she wasn't right
    b. women didn't know their right hand from their left
    c. "left" persons had clumsy notions of right and wrong
    d. such a lucrative trade required a man's delicate sense of entitlement

Part Three

1350 to 1700

CHAPTER 7

THE RENAISSANCE

The Renaissance was a rebirth of Greek and Roman culture. This was bad for women cause the Greeks' ideal was a world without women, and the Romans blamed the fall of their empire on women's shopping sacks. These dead cultures came to life when Arab scholars translated the ancient classical texts that had been buried at the bottom of the Roman sacks. It started in Italy because they thought up the word "renaissance" and didn't tell anyone else what they we're doing.

The Renaissance period was needed as a bridge between the Medieval feud-filled period and the Modern war-filled period. Without the Renaissance, filled with factional conflicts that paved the way for all-out war, the Modern period would have seemed too brutal and too abrupt, and history doesn't like hiccups. The Renaissance was useful, but not for women.

Bourgeois Beginnings

The mercantile trades and the guilds helped bring prosperity to an up-and-coming group of people called "bourgeois." To be bourgeois, you had to agree to certain social practices, like using a table knife to cut bread instead of your sword or an axe. They called these rules "norms," assuming they were normal, or "conventions" because they voted on them at Bourgeois Conventions. Bourgeois was bad for women because to be bourgeois means to be static, and women, often accused of emitting static, are quite dynamic.

Charm School

The new role for the Renaissance lady was to be "charming." Baldassare Castiglione wrote a handbook for the lady of the court, and "charm" was to be her primary objective, enabling her to entertain a man, whether a monster or milquetoast. Naturally, she'd have to give up unbecoming things, like riding horses and handling weapons. (Note: the 1st edition of the handbook had "riding weapons and handling horses"--charges of witchcraft forced the change.)

Elisabetta Gonzaga typified the new ideal. When widowed in 1508 at thirty-six years of age, an adoptive heir (chosen while her husband was still alive) assumed power instead of her. Her correspondence showed her to be as docile in adulthood as she had been as a child. She placated her father, brother, and of course her husband. People said she lacked spirit, but in a charming way.

Humanism of Renaissance: Inhuman to Women

Humanism brought Latin literacy and classical learning to daughters as well as sons of the nobility. But the Lady's influence, paramount in the medieval aristocracy, was replaced by her son's male tutors. They tore up the romantic comic books, declared chivalry dead and ushered in the classical biases against women. Men had rewritten courtly manners and tossed manners out the window.

Women and Writing

As in previous centuries, it was difficult for women to write. Isotta Nogarola, the most learned woman of the century, was told by Guarino of Verona, the head intellect of the time, that she must "become a man" if she wanted to continue writing. Ridiculed by her female friends for even trying to converse with Guarino, she stopped writing for three years, then decided to become a recluse in her own house.

Thinking and Sex Don't Mix

The price Isotta paid for being a thinking woman and keeping her respectability was isolation from other intellectuals and a lifetime of chastity. There was no role for a thinking woman who wanted to live a normal life. Who would have thought?

Marie le Jars de Gournay (1565-1645) likewise remained celibate to avoid conflict between domesticity and learning. She taught herself Latin and Greek from books and read Michel de Montaigne's *Essais*. When she met Montaigne, he became her lifetime mentor and friend. When he died in 1592, she became, at the request of Montaigne's wife, the editor of his works, issued in eight editions. She also translated the *Aeneid* into French and published her own essays and poems.

Yet she too had her career blighted by mockery, her work derided, her reputation slandered by gossip. In her feminist essays, she wrote about the equality of the sexes and insisted emphatically that the difference between men and women was due to the unequal education they received.

Mothers Forever

Unlike Marie Gournay and Guarino of Verona, most women's lives revolved around motherhood. With the high rate of miscarriage and stillbirths, a woman would be pregnant or nursing a child for most of her adult lifespan, while working without letup in the home and country fields. For peasant women, half of their children would die before the age of twenty. In England, up to the 18th century, twenty-five percent of children died in their first year.

Mothers Are Equal

It wasn't surprising that for 350 years, the main argument that women advanced for equality was based on motherhood. Mary, the mother of Jesus, was offered as the ultimate role model for women: virginity (for non-moms) and submissiveness to the feminine destiny of suffering and loss (for moms).

Margaretha Susanna von Kuntsch (1651-1716) elevated the experience of giving birth to that of the male warrior-hero in one of her poems, thus challenging the patriarchal system of values, which belittled childbirth as trivial and resented its drag on the family economy. She had fourteen children, only one of whom survived her.

Courtly Love Upside Down

The old courtly social world had vanished. The women had disappeared, both sexually and physically. In the poetry of Dante, the beloved may as well be dead, which she is. The lover in Dante's poems frustrated his own desire by rejecting even the thought of union with his beloved. Beatrice exists in his mind as a remote idea, difficult to make love with. Dante is captivated by his own inner life. He valued women in the abstract, not a good thing for women, who tend to be concrete, heavenly to be sure.

Who Needs Love?

Even this shadowy kind of romance dropped off in the 15th century renaissance of Greco-Roman art and letters. The Florentine humanists were interested only in the side of classicism that served public interests. They rejected the dominance of love in human life, along with the inwardness and reclusion of the religious, the scholar, and the love-sick poet. Testosterone was on the march, trampling anything in its way.

Plato to the Rescue

Castiglione, regarded as an important spokesman of renaissance love and manners, proposed a Platonic notion of spiritual love that separated sex and love, similar to Dante (he never actually tried it himself). He brought patriarchal notions of "women's confinement to the family," that bourgeois humanists had popularized, into the aristocracy. Now even the aristocracy was to keep love within the bonds of marriage. Of course, it was up to the women to perform this magic trick.

The First Kiss And It's Over

With the platonic definition of love as the "desire to enjoy beauty," it was bound to be downhill. The woman's role was to *inspire a man* to find supreme happiness in Divine Love. Ordinary love and beauty have been robbed of flesh and passion by this elevation. A simple kiss between the man and his beloved becomes the finale. Instead of initiating love, it becomes the end. People began to talk of the "kiss of death."

Can She or Can't She?

It became a question of whether a woman could love at all, so inconsequential had she become. Woman's beauty inspired love, but she was passive, a spectator at an event she had to attend. The agent in charge of the show was a man. Ticket sales were brisk but cold.

Can He?

On the other hand, in the 17th century, it was commonly believed that women were much more sexual than men, that they had a much greater capacity than men. Indeed, some thought them to be insatiable. Because of this, women were thought to be dangerous

Men Lose Power, Take It Out on Women

Castiglione's book, published in 1528, after the Sack of Rome--hopefully the last sack, actually called the "Sad Sack" because there was so little left to be sacked--helped the dependent noblemen boost the ego that had been trashed as the state took over their lands and power. The book's popularity spread from Italy through Europe in the 16th and 17th centuries, even though women's protest groups tried in vain to use it as firewood.

Detachment the Key

His book spoke to the weakened nobleman. Since the emerging state demanded obedience from the nobleman, Castiglione advised detachment as a coping mechanism, a way to handle his subservient position. His advice is the same whether about the love proffered a woman or about service to his master: be aloof. The noble, or "courtier," as he calls him, is to preserve his independence by avoiding even the desire for love or power. Being detached, the courtier can love and not love, serve and not serve—at the same time. Similar to today's "cool" men. Women take a hit.

Chastity's Back

Female chastity was now much more important to Renaissance noblemen as they moved into a new hereditary, dependent class. In 16th Century Italy, new laws limited membership into this class, prompting concerns with legitimacy and purity of blood. Purity tests were a bit primitive, mostly relying on color and thickness. Blue was preferred.

To help enforce the lady's chastity, a burdensome costume concealed and constrained her body while advertising her husband's rank. These voluminous dresses, some six feet across, were more effective than Chinese foot-binding at keeping women from wandering off unnoticed.

Love Subordinate to Horse

Love was now subordinate to the public concerns of the Renaissance nobleman. The personal value of love, important in feudal times for both men and women, was now the exclusive domain of the lady. The courtier's chief concern was to please his boss, the prince. A woman was secondary. Or tertiary if he had a horse.

An Aesthetic Object

With the division between personal and public life that the state was effecting, the modern relation of the separated sexes made its appearance. All the advances of Renaissance Italy helped mold the noblewoman into an *aesthetic object*. She was to be decorous, chaste, and dependent on her husband. Oh for the good ole feudal days!

CHAPTER 8

THE PROTESTANT REFORMATION

Martin Luther was a Catholic priest who wanted to get married. In his attack on clerical celibacy, he ridiculed the idea that virginity was the ideal condition for both sexes. He protested so much that they named it "protest-eth-muchism," later shortened to Protestantism. He promoted marriage for the clergy and wrote a pamphlet *On Christian Marriage*. Awed by his persuasive power, he married three years later.

The lucky woman was Katherine von Bora, who had escaped from a convent in 1523. She claimed that she could raise thousands of kronars in an early pyramid scheme by selling indulgences (she never told Martin about this).

Despite Luther's intention to "defy the devils and the pope" by marrying, no harm came to him. Any lightning bolts that came down he simply tacked onto the church door where his original manifesto was still nailed. Ambivalent about the legitimacy of sexual intercourse (he still believed it sinful), he had six children in an attempt to change his mind while wrestling with this conundrum.

Male Supremacy

Luther and his fellow Protestant leaders wanted to promote the dignity and importance of marriage but didn't want to infringe on male supremacy. A Puritan manual reminded the man to remember his superiority when he "loveth," to stay on top of things. Calvin stressed woman's biblical subordination to man.

Protestant reformers didn't like to toy with the double standard. Husbands, not wives, obtained divorces for adultery. In fact, some tried to make it a triple standard, but they didn't have the math.

Full Divorce Empties the Brothel

Nuremberg, the last important city in Germany to allow "full divorce," shut down its public brothel, the last one in Lutheran Germany, the same year. It offered no explanation.

Calvinist Geneva: Against Sex

Edicts were passed in 1566 requiring equal punishments for men and women for misconduct: prison terms with a diet of bread and water for fornication; banishment for adultery with an unmarried person; and death for adultery between two married persons (threesomes were smoked outright). But only women were executed for adultery. Male citizens managed to escape banishment for adulteries committed with servants. Calvin blamed women for anything he could think, and he thought a lot.

Patriarchal Clampdown

In an attempt to stop the kids from eloping and to safeguard patriarchal privileges, protestant theologians demanded two adult witnesses as a precondition for a valid betrothal and required a church ceremony for a valid marriage. Catholics followed suit, and Catholic governments implemented the changes. Roman Copy-Caths.

God Will Talk Back to Women

Women were told that they could speak to God and that He'd speak back to them, just as he did to men. According to Luther, this gift was open to both men and women. But in practice, as orthodoxy hardened into the old familiar shapes, women had to turn to left-wing groups of the Reformation to find acceptance of their voice, such as the Anabaptists, Quakers, and Pietism. And of course early talk-radio.

Woman Preachers

In 17th -century England, various religious sects separated from the Church of England. Some featured women as lay preachers. The first famous speaker was Anne Hutchinson, leader of the Antinomians in Massachusetts, who thought the Puritans were too legalistic. The Antinomians believed you could get into heaven without working at it: if you had faith in your beliefs or beliefs in your faith, you were in. Anne had religious meetings at her house and took issue with some of the Puritan ideas and the preachers.

Unfortunately she lived across the street from Governor Winthrop who wasn't invited. He didn't think a woman had the authority to be teaching anybody, especially men, so he banished her from the colony. The church ministers followed suit and excommunicated her. When she had a miscarriage, they wagged their fingers and said God was punishing her.

Women Take on the Bible

Women continued to offer their own interpretation of scripture to offset the lop-sided, women-hating point of view offered by men. In the 15th -century, two women offered fresh insights. Christine de Pizan (1365-1430) wrote *The Book of the City of the Ladies* in 1405, a spirited defense of women. She pointed out that Eve surpassed Adam by being born of nobler stuff: Adam from dirt, Eve from short ribs. And Original

Sin was not all that bad since human nature was lifted higher as a result of Mary giving birth to Jesus, than it was lowered cause of Eve's sin. Good thing she sinned.

Isotta Nogarola (1416-1466) dealt with Adam and Eve's responsibility for the fall differently. According to her, Eve was weaker by nature than Adam, and therefore less culpable for assenting to the "wise" snake. Adam, created with perfect knowledge and understanding, should have known better than to listen to the faulty logic of the imperfect, non-thinking Eve. Thomas Aquinas was glad to be dead.

Friendly Quakes

But women didn't start moving up till after the English Civil War. The Quakers, or Society of Friends, were founded in 1648. Called "Quakers" because of the shakes they went into when arrested, they famously tried to make friends with anybody they met. Margaret Fell, an early Quaker, published a work on *Women's Speaking Justified*, in which she argued that women had a mouth. Like most prominent Quakers, she spent long periods in prison. Quakers were definitely friends of women.

Women and the Catholic Reformation

It wasn't long before Rome realized reformations pushed up stocks and declared its own Initial Papal Offering, which immediately doubled dividends on Novenas. They called theirs the Counter-Reformation because its main feature was the abolition of over-the-counter sales of indulgences.

Trent Says No to Concubines for Priests

The Catholic Counter-Reformation was no better for women than the original Reformation. The Council of Trent (1545-1563) reaffirmed clerical celibacy, and viciously attacked concubines, still found among twenty-percent of the parish clergy in Luxembourg as late as 1580. The priests who had the concubines were generally less chased than their mistresses.

Nuns Let Out

Rome grudgingly let the nuns loose, exposing them to life beyond the walls of the nunnery. Church authorities tolerated their engagement in nursing and education. These were significant innovations for women in early modern Europe where women were confined to the kitchen, only let out to empty the slop bucket.

Convents: Dumping Grounds or Retreats for Casanova

Convents continued, despite reform attempts by bishops, to be dumping grounds for surplus daughters of Catholic aristocrats. This led to bouts of collective frenzy, diagnosed as "demonic possession," in some 17th -century convents in France and Spain. It also led to a noticeable laxity in 18th -century convents where Casanova, known for his preying ability, spent a lot of time. He preyed, fooled around and increased his fame. He had many converts.

Brothels and Women

During the Middle Ages, most large cities and many smaller ones had opened one or more municipal brothels. They hired a brothel manager and prostitutes, and they passed regulations concerning women and their customers. They protected the women from violence and overexploitation, and saw it as a necessary service for journeyman and out-of-town visitors. In–towners were often seen impersonating out-of-towners, pretending to be lost.

Women Discriminated Against

Attitudes changed during the Reformation period, and both Protestant and Catholics pushed the "Triumph of Lent." This was an attempt to control the free-spirited frivolity and sexual license associated with Carnival in 16th -century Europe. This reform movement affected women through the drive to close public brothels, which began in Lutheran Germany between 1530 and 1560. Prostitutes had to wear distinctive clothing: loose togas with a giant "P" on the front and back, and couldn't appear in public. In Catholic Europe, brothels disappeared last in the Mediterranean region. The walled prostitutes' quarter of Valencia, voted #1 in Frommer's Travel Guide, survived until 1635.

CHAPTER 9

OUT WITH PAGANISM, IN WITH THE DEVIL

The reformations ended Christianity's thousand-year year attempt to assimilate paganism. Religious authorities now mounted a massive attack on "idolatry," the worship of false gods and superstition. If you were dyslexic and made the sign-of-the-cross backwards, you might be accused of both superstition and idolatry. Any "magical activities" practiced by old women could be deemed superstitious. There goes the head.

Here Comes the Devil

The early catechisms used by Martin Luther, as well as St. Peter Canasius, a Jesuit, were more about the Devil than about Jesus. This early imprinting on children would later result in adults who ruthlessly persecuted and executed "witches." The Devil was particularly interested in women, and they were said to be interested in Him. The 16th century was filled with fear of the Devil. The pagan associations with devil-worship, demonic possession, and witchcraft, all focused on women, especially single women and single mothers. Germany cranked out an amazing number of *teufelbucher*, or works about the Devil. The best-seller was titled: *Terrorist Devils Hijack Women's Broomstream Plane.*

Witch Hunts

All over Europe, women were put to death for the quasi-religious crime of being a witch. Most "witches" lived in small villages, surrounded by suspicious neighbors. The persecution lasted from 1560-1670. More than 100,000 people went on trial, with a third being put to death. In a tiny southwestern corner of Germany (Baden-Wurttemberg), records show about 3,500 deaths for witchcraft, most of them women.

Joan of Arc—Early Gender Victim

Joan of Arc, the Maid of Orleans, claimed she heard heavenly voices telling her to lead the French army against the English king and bring back the Dauphin, Charles, to be crowned king of France. This she did, having donned a full suit of armor and leading the troops to victory. But once Charles was on the throne, Joan was turned over to the enemy. She was accused of wearing men's clothes, of "acting against nature." Charged with demonic possession, she was burned at the stake in 1431.When her clothes wouldn't burn, they knew they'd done the right thing.

She Killed a Cow

Jeanette Clerc's trial was rapid. The wife of a peasant, she lived in a little hamlet near Geneva. She was arrested in 1539 because her neighbor's cow died suddenly after Jeanette fed it some herbs. Other accusations followed, the most serious: that she killed one of her husband's relatives years before by throwing "diabolical powder" in his face. DNA tests revealed the powder to be from a pre-historic goat.

Within two weeks, they had extracted a complete confession from her. She'd "become a witch in a fit of rage after losing a new pair of shoes." She rode on the devil's back (his name was Simon) to the synagogue and there made love to him, "in the rear like animals." The Republic of Geneva beheaded her and confiscated her property. But they returned her shoes, now charcoal-stained, which the witch had stolen.

Riding on Brooms

The first illustration of a female witch riding on a broomstick (1440) appeared in a poem that ridiculed the belief in witchcraft, but the image stuck. And witches never did convert to plane travel.

Mal for Women

The *Malleus Maleficarum*, published in 1486 by two German Dominicans, was the bible for inquisitions. Church authorities had already tried fifty women for witchcraft; all but two of the witches were women. Germany was the center of the witch craze, a bad place for women in broom manufacture. Women now used rags to sweep floors and boycotted broom stores.

The *Malleus* text explains why women were especially prone to witchcraft: they were more credulous, more impressionable, and had slippery tongues (they had to tell other women what they learned from the evil arts). Furthermore, drawing on the traditional belief in women's greater sexual appetite, it argued that, "women's insatiable lust leads them to accept even the Devil as a lover."

Better to be Stupid

"Educated" people in England believed that women's uncontrollable sexuality deprived them of the ability to reason. Since women's sex drive increased with age, older, unmarried women were seen as potential seductresses, willing to do anything to satisfy their sexual urges. The devil, if accepted by them, promised sexual satisfaction. The uneducated knew better.

Witches in the American Colonies

Witchcraft persecution soared in popularity throughout the Puritan colonies, but it skyrocketed in Salem in 1693. Of the two-hundred people accused in the village of Salem, three-fourths of them were women, as were fifteen of the twenty executed. A run on broomsticks forced the nascent housing industry to turn to mud, match-makers to plastic.

The Economics of Witchcraft

Not surprisingly, witchcraft had an economic twist. Widowed women without brothers or sons, especially if they had property, were more likely to be targeted as witches. Women stood in the way of the orderly transfer of property from one generation of males to the next. If the husband was still alive and over forty (and unlikely to produce heirs), the woman might be scrutinized more carefully for signs of witchcraft. Does she wear a skirt? In fact, witchcraft accusations were rarely taken seriously until the accused stopped having kids. With the Sterilization-of-Brooms Act in 1696, even witches went childless.

Loss of Property

Elinor Hollingworth, who lost her merchant husband at sea in 1677, was accused of witchcraft after she had paid off her husband's debts and salvaged his warehouse and tavern business. The magistrate paid little attention to the accusations by the wife of a Gloucester mariner until Elinor's son William died. Elinor, seeing the script unraveling, deeded her whole estate to her daughter, Mary English, in 1685. But that wasn't the end of it. They now accused Elinor's daughter Mary of witchcraft, as well as her husband Phillip. Mary and Phillip fled to the safety of New York, but "flight" was the legal equivalent of conviction, and their property was confiscated.

Stillborn or Infanticide?

Prior to the 16th century, stillborn death was not unusual, and few women had been prosecuted for infanticide. But new laws in France and England placed the burden of proof in cases of newborn death on the defendants, mostly mothers of illegitimate children.

Governments mounted a crusade against unwed mothers charged with infanticide. Convictions rates were very high. Trials and executions for infanticide multiplied in the 16th and 17th centuries, just when witch-hunting peaked. The Church's beliefs about the Devil justified their savagery toward these women.

State Takes Over

The male hysteria about witchcraft and infanticide resulted from the increased interference of public institutions in daily life. The state enforced church attendance, the clergy preached obedience to civil authorities, and both tried to out-do each other in regulating everybody's behavior. Pressure to walk straight in Germany led to the outlawing of circles, and the Church in France restricted the height bread could rise, claiming host preferences.

Fear Behind the Walls

Fear played a part as well. People peered at their neighbors behind walled towns and fortified castles. Anything that looked suspicious might be judged superstitious. Making the sign-of-the-cross backwards might be devilish or lewd. Old women with deviant dreams were scapegoats in this obsession with the Devil. And men were clean as a whistle, given extra indulgences for turning in women to the authorities.

Patriarchy: the Usual Suspect

Patriarchal thinking determined which group of women would become the victims. Their thoughts led right to the doors of lower-class women who lived outside male supervision: accused witches were largely widows; infanticide defendants were single women. Their "unnatural" condition aroused suspicion and fear. All that was needed was a tip from a "friendly neighbor."

Women Need a Master

In the 16th century, civic and religious authorities decided to crack down on women living independently. They were worried about public order and morality. With "The Triumph of Lent," they expanded "Sumptuary Laws." These laws attempted to regulate morality by making it more expensive to be naughty. They limited how much you could spend on a dress or push-up bra, restricted public dances and carnivals, and prohibited gambling and prostitution.

Defer Gratification

Protestantism wrecked havoc on "Merrie Old England." The idea was to curb your drinking, rise before the sun, work till dark and be glad for what you get. The middle classes had to learn to save and defer pleasure. The lower classes had to be molded into a disciplined, factory-ready working class. The new industries demanded labor year round. Louis XIV of France reduced the number of saints' days from several hundred a year to ninety-two (*Dancing in the Streets*).

Governments toughened laws against vagrants. There were too many footloose people wandering about without a master: actors, beggars, musicians, mercenary soldiers and servants between jobs who couldn't use the Internet. They were not part of a male-run household, the desired unit of social control. Women who lived alone as "masterless," were lumped together with vagrants and migrants and viewed with increasing suspicion and hostility. The authorities made it difficult for a woman to be economically independent. A subsistence wage, enough to support herself and her family was recommended. She could work at McDonald's but not at Piggily-Wiggily.

Unmarried Women Can't Move

In Germany and France, there were laws that forbade unmarried women from moving into cities, required widows to move in with one of their male children, and obliged unmarried women to move in with a male relative or employer. In Catholic areas, unmarried women not living under strict cloister were suspected of being aliens from Mars.

In the American Colonies

In the Colonies, unattached women were even more suspect than in England. But the Native population had no problem with widows. They simply attached themselves to the nearest wigwam, where they were quite welcome. Native American families were a bit more flexible than that of the colonials, whose chief occupation was manufacturing rules and regulations.

Hysteria and Demonic Possession

There was particular concern about the mental state of nuns in the 17th century. Some people saw a similarity between the symptoms of hysteria and those of demonic possession; both shared some of the same sexual manifestations. See Appendix for erotic examples.

Can't Keep that Womb Down

Even in the 17th century, most authors still believed that hysteria was brought on by the uterus traveling where it wasn't supposed to go. A travel ban didn't work. Treatment consisted in bringing the woman's fluids down by means of crisis intervention, culminating in hysterical paroxysm. That would put the uterus back in its place. And the woman could relax.

Hysteria Rampant

Hysteria was considered common and chronic in women, the most common disease except for fever. The famous physician Thomas

Sydenham claimed that it was responsible for one sixth of all human maladies. William Harvey in 1653 called it a terrible scourge caused by disorders of menstruation and sexual malfunction.

Chapter 10

Women Get the Pink Slip

In the medieval economy, the household was the basic unit of production, like a mini-factory. Even peasant families participated. They might sell extra chickens at the open market and use the proceeds to buy condiments to spice up their dreary lives.

The urban household might also include servants, journeymen and apprentices of the master who would live at the house with his wife and children. They were all part of the production and distribution of their product, whether they were spinning indulgences, weaving rosary beads or sewing fancy garters, and they all stood to benefit from good sales. Labor was not divided by gender or by the status of members of the household. Whoever spun best got the job. This economy was good for women.

Craft Guilds Come to Town

In the 13th and 14th centuries, "craft guilds" were set up in cities to organize and regulate production and to set standards for the finished product. There might be a hundred or more different guilds in a city, from Cloth-spinning Guilds to Toothpick Guilds to the ever-popular, Gilding-of-the-Lily Guilds.

Early Capitalism in Western Europe

A new economic organization appeared in the late Middle Ages. It began among merchants who traded luxury goods in the international marketplace, like spice and silks. They made enormous profits, and the smell of money attracted non-family investors. As they grew in size, they had to hire outside help. *These laborers were paid wages rather than a share of the profit. Capitalism had begun and would turn out to be a disaster for women.* As an abstract system, utilizing an abstraction, capital, it created an invisible barrier, shielding its effects from the cause.

Capitalism Gives Women Pink Slip

Before capitalism, work was defined as "activities performed to support and sustain one's self and one's family." Domestic and productive tasks were both considered work, and all women could correctly be called "working women." Under capitalism, work was defined as "an activity for which one was paid." Overnight, the number of women "workers" plummeted. The majority of women became "unemployed."

Women: Lazy at Home

Domestic tasks and childrearing were not considered work unless they were done for wages. Fast forward to the German industrial code of 1869, and we find that women who spun, washed, ironed or knitted in their own homes were not considered "workers" (not eligible for pensions or wages), but male shoemakers or tailors who worked in their homes were considered "workers." Nothing women did at home was truly work. This idea, started back then, would continue into modern times, and men still think it's "work" if they put on their socks, "play" if women have to darn or iron them.

Too Many Women

In medieval and early modern cities, with a large surplus of women (from 10-20% more women than men), a lot of urban women couldn't choose marriage as a career even if they were foolish enough.

Dowry Stakes Raised

In such a market, middle-class and upper-class women were expected to provide dowries to their husbands, so marriages were often delayed till they could afford a proper dowry. A poor woman would have to work for years, as a maid or pieceworker, to be able to buy bedding or a Bendix washer as dower. Dowries were not in women's best interests.

Many women lived alone or in households headed by women. Most were widows, but a large percentage were young women who hadn't yet married. Households of widows and unmarried women made up almost one-third of all households in many cities. "Household" didn't mean a house. It usually meant a rented room, cellar, or attic. Or doghouse, vacated when the dog moved on.

From Guilds to Spinning their Wheels

In the 16th century, men ran the craft guilds, but a large number of women worked in them. In a typical setting, bread and clothing were purchased, rather than made at home, so that the women could spend time in production rather than housework.

In the workshop, the master's wife sold the goods, collected debts, and kept the books. If the master craftsman died, the widow could carry on as long as she remained unmarried, depending on the century.

By the Century

In the 13th century, no problem: even in iron-making and roofing, the widow could carry on without the husband. By the mid-15th century, widows could only finish work that her husband had already begun. By the mid-16th century, widows couldn't hire anybody new, and sometimes couldn't keep the workers they had. They could barely survive: tax records show that more than two-thirds of widows were in the poorest income category. By the 17th century, widows tended to sell the shop upon the death of the husband. In the 18th century, they sold the shop before he died, just to stay ahead of the game.

As women were shut out of the guilds, they began to produce cheap and simple items like soap, candles, thimbles, brooms, combs, wooden bowls and spoons, toasters and hair dryers (for the aristocrats). These were not regulated by the guilds, and they could do this after their regular day time job, for example working in the countryside fields or as laundresses in town.

Let's Be Seamstresses

City councils, eager to get women off "poor relief," encouraged seamstressing. Small endowments provided poor girls with training, as did orphanages.

Cheap, for Women Only

Cloth production was a significant source of employment for both rural and urban women. Guilds sometimes would allow women to produce cheaper cloth made specifically for women's clothing. A popular urban myth, never explained, was that expensive cloth would stain a woman's virtue.

Everybody Spins

City councils expected women to keep spinning while in jail, prostitutes to spin between customers. Wealth or education was no obstacle. When James I of England was presented with a prospective bride, someone who could speak and write Latin, Greek and Hebrew, his first question was: Can she spin? In Memmingen, a suicidal woman was to be chained to her hospital bed in such a way so that she could still spin. With so many women spinning, wages were kept low. Women were spun badly by spinning, both in the work field and in the mine field of "information."

Women and Markets

The open-air market was at the center of every city, and women were the market. They conducted almost all of the retail distribution of food, used clothing, household articles and liquor. They were also the majority of customers. Women got their gossip and news at the market, the church, and the neighborhood water well. Men gathered to gossip in taverns, slurring the news.

Sales

Most women in sales, from 1300 to 1700, sold goods from a basket they carried or from a small stand in the marketplace. The city government regulated the prices, hours of operation, and the variety of produce or goods each woman could offer. In the latter 16th century, some cities tried to keep young females from having a stand, preferring to see them work as maids. They'd be less likely to be independent.

Anna Didn't Like Rules

Anna Weyland appeared before the Stasbourg city council many times over a thirty-year period. Some of the charges: illegally selling herring, refusing to sell herring unless a customer also bought dried cod, selling herring below price, selling candles below price, using children to sell candles, selling candles that were underweight, and selling candied candles candidly.

When she told the council that she didn't intend to obey their ordinances, they threatened to "pinch her with glowing tongs and throw her in the water" if she didn't obey. She and her husband shuttered the shop and declared bankruptcy.

Beer for Better Breasts

Women were also heavily involved in making beer and running taverns. Female brewers in Munich also took care of a woman in childbirth, nursing her during her delivery. They plied her with plenty of beer to get her back on her feet again and to fill her breasts with milk. The babies slept between hiccups. When distilling was discovered in the 16th century, women distilled and sold brandy.

Rags and Riches

But the richest and most powerful women were those selling used merchandise. They operated as pawnbrokers and as appraisers, helping those who were selling merchandise to pay off debts to creditors. Their businesses were small, but they didn't hesitate to bring people to court, often over slander and defamation. They called other women and men names—thief, whore and arsehole—and they refused to apologize until it reached the city's highest court. In a case in Strasbourg, a woman didn't utter the formulaic "I know nothing but good and honor about this person," until she was in prison for three weeks on bread and water.

Chapter 11

At Your Service, Naturally

Most women were employed in "services." Many of these occupations were stereotyped as "natural" for women. They required little training, the hours could be flexible, and they were extensions of what women did anyway: cooking, cleaning, childcare, nursing the sick, caring for the elderly, and running the show. For these reasons, women in this sector were undervalued and rarely protested to get more money.

Women as Hospital CEOs

When city governments took over hospitals, orphanages and pest-houses from the religious branch, they appointed women to staff them, from janitors to administrators. The mistress or "keeper" was the CEO, responsible for the budget outlay, kitchen staffing and procedures, and making sure patients received what they needed.

All the employees of the hospital had to swear an oath of loyalty and agree to follow all council directives. The hospital was seen as a family, the mother (mistress) taking care of her children. Therefore, these women, no matter what their responsibilities, were not considered professionals. They were poorly paid, often receiving little more than board and room. City orphanages were also modeled after the family, with a married couple in charge.

Wet-Nursing

Infants, not admitted to orphanages, were given to wet nurses. Wet-nursing provided employment for women whose own infants made other work difficult.

Wet-nursing was not a male concern till the 18th century when considerations of class made families reluctant to place their charges with poorer women. They feared disease and stale milk.

Pest-Houses

Those with contagious diseases—the plague, leprosy or smallpox—were consigned to small pest-houses outside the city. These pest-houses naturally employed women, usually on a short-term basis. The women in charge simply tried to keep patients fed and clean until they died. Medical knowledge being what it was, women were instructed to simply air out the sheets and clothing of dead patients, then reuse them as bandages for new arrivals. They didn't stay long.

Midwifery

This was the most important occupation open to women. Midwives handled all births, from the very poor to the nobility. Few male doctors worked in obstetrics and gynecology until the 18th century. City councils paid midwives an annual salary to take care of poor women and, in the 15th century, they appointed upper-class women to oversee the midwives and license them. Midwifery was the only field where an organized hierarchy of women operated similar to that of men in a craft guild or in city government.

Who's the Father?

A midwife learned through an apprenticeship, passed an examination, took an oath and received a license. Her oaths required her to perform emergency baptisms if she felt the child might die. She had to report illegitimate children and try to discover the identity of the father, sometimes during the pain of birth. If the mother-to-be didn't remember the father's name, the midwife might forget to extract the baby. The midwife also had to swear not to perform abortions or to repeat superstitions.

Women as Physicians

Women faced no opposition working in hospitals. Outside the hospital was another matter. This was the male domain of physicians, barber-surgeons and apothecaries. Women were listed as physicians up to the late 15th century, but after that, the title required medical training at a university. That path was closed to women.

Sharp lines began to divide those "professionals" who had received formal training (men) and those who simply practiced on their own (women). The former convinced governments to forbid "women and other untrained people" to practice medicine, and they gradually disappeared from public records.

Women's Skills from the Devil

Some women were allowed to handle minor problems like skin diseases and boils if they promised not to charge too much. But barber-surgeons objected even to this. They complained that their own profession was irreparably damaged if any women did the same work as they did. Indeed, they suggested that women's skills must be diabolical, for God would not give such medical expertise to a woman. Barber-surgeons traveled by broomstick.

Appraisers and Beaters Out, Domestics In

During the 16th century, cities began to demand more formal legal language in appraisals, one of women's specialties. With little formal education, women found it hard to write out an acceptable inventory of goods. Later, appraisers became city officials, and that ended this career path for women. Formal education was bad for women cause they couldn't get it.

Other service work for women: running small schools, inspecting milk, and serving as gatekeepers and toll-collectors, all paid poorly. Ditto for work as day laborers in construction or in harvesting, where women were paid one-half the wages of adult males.

Public Baths Out of Style

Up to the 16th century, all major cities had public baths. Women served as bath attendants, washing customers' hair and bodies, trimming nails, and beating them with branches to improve circulation. Gradually the baths became less popular as people no longer celebrated weddings, christenings, and business agreements with a group bath as they had in the Middle Ages. Additionally, city councils now prohibited mixed-sex bathing out of public morality concerns, and most public baths were forced to close.

Domestics on the Rise

Domestics continued to make up the biggest employee group. By the 17th century, a woman who worked outside the home was likely to work as a servant in someone else's house. Fifteen to twenty-percent of the population of cities was made up of domestic servants. Servants' duties were more and more specialized and divided by gender, unlike the Middle Ages when both men and women cooked, cleaned and bottle-washed. Now boys handled stable chores, women and girls were responsible for the kitchen and interior household. At least they received equal pay, next to nothing.

Don't Get Too Uppity

City officials did their best to regulate the conduct, salaries and social activities of servants once they were hired. They were discouraged from getting married, from setting up house on their own, or from working on their own as day laborers. The idea was to keep them dependent, under the control of a master. For this reason, wages were limited. Officials in Stuttgart were horrified that servants wanted wages in addition to room and board.

If You Can't Afford It, Don't Wear It

In the late 16th and 17th centuries, there were stricter rules against servants. Employers no longer trusted them. New consumptive laws established clear class distinctions: servants could not wear fancy clothing or jewelry even if they were gifts from the employer.

Meanwhile Among the Primitives in Canada

A Jesuit, Paul Le Jeune, was Superior of the French mission at Quebec in 1632. He wintered with the Montagnais-Naskapi Indians. He was horrified at what he saw: indulgent parents, independent women, divorced men and women, men with two wives, and no formal leaders. It was a peripatetic, relaxed culture in which women enjoyed a high economic and social status. Father Le Jeune taught them discipline for children, lifetime monogamy, male authority, and female obedience. Ten years later, wife-beating had begun in the tribe (*Anatomy of Love*, Fisher, 1994). The Roman Catholic Church had succeeded once again.

And in the Colonies

The missionaries were also hard at work on the Native population in New England. The Native Americans were primitive in their morals and manners. The evangelists had the most success with the women, urging them to introduce prayer and order into the tribe. The evangelists' challenge was to convince the wives to *reform their husbands into becoming masters over them.* Wife-beating was not mentioned as a fringe benefit.

But conversion was not working. The Indians continued to prefer their own "primitive" way of life. After 1676, the missionaries emphasized servitude (a sort of slavery-lite) in order to bring English ways into their lives, to civilize them, trivialize them.

Bastardy

When women gave birth to bastards, they were to blame; men were off the hook. In 1657, Jane Pauldin told the Maryland Provincial Court that John Newton, a planter, came to her when his wife was abroad and seduced her "to be dishonest with him." She was given thirty lashes on her bare-back for her confession. He was slapped on the wrist.

Worse still if a servant had a bastard by the master. Most of the time this was not reported. But some courts ruled that the woman in question had to serve two extra years to make up for her evil and her down-time. These cases were reported by the master since it was in his interest. When this seemed too beneficial for the master (and all-of-a-sudden there was a rash of reporting), the woman was "loaned out" to the parish to work for two years instead of working for the master.

Wagging Tongues, Off the Ears

Next to bastardy, slander was the most common offence of colonial women. Lacking crops (fines were paid in tobacco), women had to be whipped or worse. Blanch Howell, a Maryland matron, gave false testimony about the ownership of a cow. She was condemned to stand in a pillory and had to forfeit her ears.

Public Ducking for Women

Each county had to have a ducking machine, along with branding irons, stocks, a pillory post and a whipping post. A public ducking was the usual treatment for the sin of slandering. Rubber duckies were given out to women who exceeded three minutes.

You Have the right to Remain Silent

As in England, colonial women were without political rights and were legal nonentities. However, single women were considered competent for purposes of private law, but as soon as they were married, the husband took over as lord and head. Runaway wives were treated the same as runaway slaves: an ad in the paper alerted the public not to break the law by helping them in any way, and a reward was offered for their return.

Okay to Beat Her But Not Damage Permanently

Husbands were allowed to administer corporal punishment to their wives, but they were not entitled to inflict permanent injury or death to their beloved spouses. Unfortunately, many of them got carried away, and the courts sometimes had to separate them, putting them in separate houses (or separate states), if her life was in danger.

Can't Keep the Kids

Even when forcefully separated due to the husband's brutal and licentious behavior, the mother had no legal right over her children. English law gave the father authority over the children even after his death. By his will or deed, he could dispose of living children, as well as a child still in her womb. The father could appoint his wife as guardian with the stipulation that her guardianship be terminated if she remarried. He would take over from the grave.

Can't Keep the Clothes

A husband bequeathed his wife *her own clothing*, jewels and other intimate personal articles. Any personal property or income of hers belonged to him, including wages earned by her. After he gave her the weekly allowance, he promptly collected it. The Reverend Casper Stoever added a catch: if his wife slandered him after he died, everything would be taken from her, including the clothes on her body. She could keep the memories.

A Wife's Duties

The first duty of a wife is to obey her husband. This subjection is punishment laid upon wives for Eve's disobedience. Their obedience makes up for Eve's original disobedience. Marriage is the natural state for a woman since the purpose of her existence is to continue the human species and to be a helpmate to her husband. Marriage was badly conceived for women.

Feminine Virtues

All the marriage manuals of the day carried the party line, and the party was Man. As helpmate, she was to try to please him with her every word and action, he being the lord. Meekness was highly favored and natural, given her innate inferiority. A humble distrust of herself scored many points. Some women were so highly developed in mistrust and humility that they became invisible, and husbands had to advertise for them. They were lost in crowds, not found till the smoke cleared. Wit was also bad for women; they had little of it to spare anyway. Curiosity was not good, but ignorance was highly prized. Their chatter should be about mundane stuff, the minutiae they knew so well.

Drunk? Put Him to Bed

If her husband comes home sloshed, she's to make up a soft bed for him and guide him gently to it, being glad that he's not perfect. If she finds out about his infidelity, she's to conceal her knowledge of it, happy that she doesn't need to be suspicious anymore (*The Ladies Calling,* R. Allestree, 1673). She could rejoice each time he betrayed her, more secure in her knowledge.

If He's Incompetent

If the husband happens to be a nincompoop, the wife must cover for him. Fake it. Pretend that he's in charge of the store even if you're the proprietor, bookkeeper and salesperson (and he's on his deathbed). Make it look like he's calling the shots.

Lord Halifax, in his book, *The Lady's New Year's Gift, or, Advice to a Daughter* (1688), so popular in England that it ran through fifteen editions between 1688 and 1765, explained inequality between the sexes this way:

> *Women were short-changed when it came to reason. Men, being the "Law Givers," were given more reason. Women were more endowed with "Compliance" to help them perform their Duties, taking care of him and having babies.*

Unpublished was the "Daughter's Response to His Advice."

Calling All Ladies

In *The Ladies Calling*, the final authority for over 100 years on the nature and duties of women in the United States, women were told to beware of "mischievous curiosity" and to pretend ignorance regarding "Indecent things." And they shouldn't read romances, which aroused "amorous passions." Better to pray, do needlework, and reflect on their ignorance. Bring on the kids.

Speaking of Kids

Around 1700 there were ten or twelve kids in most of the two-hundred and fifty families in Charles Town. Lord Adam Gordon said of the Virginians: they married early and were "great Breeders." John and Thomasine Thruston had sixteen children in sixteen years. Already a widow with three kids when she married John, Thomasine died thirteen days after her 19th child was born. A month later, John married again and had eight more kids. Then he disappeared down a rabbit hole.

Court-ordered Cross-Dressing

Thomasine Hall, christened and raised as a girl in England, changed her clothes to fight in a war as a man, then donned her feminine attire to support herself by doing needlework after the war. Once again, she changed back to men's clothes, coming to Virginia in 1627 as Thomas Hall.

Thomasine Hall dressed as a woman in Virginia and worked as a maidservant. On two different occasions, three women examined Thomasine's body and concluded he was a man. The local commander, Captain Basse, concluded Thomasine Hall was female and ordered him to put on "weomans apparel." The highest judicial court then heard the case and accepted T's self-definition, that he/she was both male and female. They ordered Thomas Hall to dress in men's clothes except for his head on which would be a bonnet and forehead cloth, and he was also to wear an apron. Plus a 10-gallon hat under the bonnet, so as not to look suspicious.

SUMMARY

Feudal noblewomen lost the last vestiges of their former power, and were sent off to Charm School to learn how to become aesthetic objects at home. Men, weakened by their loss of land to the State, puffed up their chests in front of women, and became even more aloof.

After the Reformation, the churches continued their indulgence in futility, now focusing on witches and the devil. Particularly susceptible were widows and single women, especially if property was involved.

With the beginnings of capitalism, women were now "unemployed," though they still did the same work at home as before. Pushed out of the medical field, they were encouraged to become seamstresses, the rage occupation of the day (prostitutes were urged to practice between tricks). And women were given field manuals on "How to be virtuous," and "How to prop up the poor, crest-fallen guy."

Quiz #3

1. Martin Luther founded Protestantism to:
   a. get into indulgences
   b. indulge his propensity for run-away nuns
   c. practice tacking up manifestoes

2. They shut down brothels because:
   a. The "locals" kept getting lost
   b. religious reformers were attacked by fits of the Morality Pest
   c. women who worked there spun customers instead of clothes

3. Quakers got their name from:
   a. the quaking sound they made when arrested
   b. the shaking fit they contracted when contacted from above
   c. the quacking routine they went into with friends for laughs

4. The Counter-Reformation by Rome was:
   a. an excuse to attend an 18-year-long council at the Trent Resort, expenses paid, by church dignitaries to discuss price supports for indulgences
   b. an excuse to let the nuns out to feed on the open grasses
   c. an attempt to stop over-the-counter novenas

5. Pagans were feared because:
   a. they knew more spells
   b. they had more gods
   c. their gods were more fun

6. Joan of Arc was executed for:
   a. forgetting to change her clothes on time
   b. thinking it was Carnival
   c. having no sense of fashion
   d. making men more insecure than they already were

7. Witch hunts were started because:
   a. women who owned property rode to work on brooms
   b. men believed women to be too sexy
   c. men thought that the Devil had a way with women

8. The Devil was more popular than Jesus because:
   a. he drove a hard bargain
   b. he was a favorite with the catechism crowd
   c. he was sexier

9. The natives were thought to be "primitive" because:
   a. they hadn't discovered advanced wife-beating
   b. the women were considered to be human beings
   c. the children were treated as human beings
   d. they enjoyed life too much

10. If a woman was guilty of slander
   a. she had to give up her rubber ducky
   b. she got a free ride on the ducking machine
   c. she had to listen to hip-hop till her ears flapped off.

11. The virtuous colonial woman:
   a. acted dumb to show how smart she was
   b. pretended her master was giving the orders at his funeral
   c. never asked "why" because she hadn't acquired reason

12. If a woman found out her husband was stepping out, she should:
   a. be glad that her suspicions were correct
   b. rejoice that he, too, has faults
   c. not let on lest he feel guilty
   d. buy another rubber ducky

Part Four

1700 to 1900

CHAPTER 12

THE ENLIGHTENMENT

It was France's turn for something big. Germany had the Reformation. Italy sponsored the Renaissance. France now hosted the Enlightenment. They assembled a team of thinkers called "philosophes," renowned the world over for their swifter and deeper thoughts: Voltaire, Montesquieu, Diderot and Rousseau.

Voltaire and Montesquieu thought the domestic subordination of women was ordained by Nature, if not by God himself. Diderot was famous for the first *Encyclopedie*, which contained thirty-one articles about "woman" (all by men). And Rousseau believed that women, along with sex and love, were insoluble problems. According to him, women, not quite "imperfect men," were just too difficult to deal with. This was the best the Endarkenment had to offer.

If You Don't Like the Product

The relations of men and women, always contentious, were now placed under the scrutinizing lens of Reason. William Alexander, in the *History of Women* (1776), explained that womanhood was of man's making, and if men didn't like the "product," they should look to the producers, themselves. As "products" of their own patriarchal system, men should be happy with the results. They got the women they deserved (*Flesh in the Age of Reason*, Porter, 2003).

Private Ownership: Boon to Women

Other writers, who shall go unmentioned, concluded that the private ownership of women, conferred by marriage, was a "milestone of progress," a huge advance over that of "savages." Who weren't advanced in ownership and its attendant privileges.

Man Ascendant

Humans (meaning "men") were definitely on top. The "individual" (meaning male) was now the source and purpose of knowledge, not God. The revolutionary doctrines of the "rights of man" and the "rights of the citizen" were now circulating in all the lending libraries of the leading male minds of the time. "Faith" and "Religion" were now subpoenaed to testify as to their truth and validity. If not up to it, out they went. This could have been good for women. Unfortunately men were locked up when it came to women.

The pope, who once persecuted the heathen for superstitious beliefs, was now on the defensive, attempting to justify the Church's weird beliefs about virgin birth, mail-order indulgences and packed "energy wafers" that contained a person by virtue of some mumbo-jumbo incantations. These reason-obsessed "philosophes" dismissed the whole package as "popery." Reason now took center stage, pontificating on knowledge and society. Women were still behind the stage, entangled in the ropes and props.

Education for Girls

It seemed pointless to educate girls, other than for motherhood, since they were not to join the priestly, military or civic castes. They should learn to sew and bow. And, come to think of it, they didn't have a mind for education. Aristotle knew that.

Up to 1700, there were fewer than 300 learned women in Western Europe (*Creation of Feminine Consciousness*, Lerner, 1993). Most of these were from the nobility or the nunnery. Given that women were thought to have defective minds, they were not encouraged to think. Their thoughts might come out crooked or warped.

Women and Salons

Elite French women pioneered the idea of "salons" (later exported to America as saloons). These were drawing rooms on wealthy homes where they drew other like-minded ladies to encourage culture and civility. They taught men table manners, how to use a fork instead of a pitchfork for example, and how to be courteous in the presence of a lady: use a spittoon, not the hem of her dress. The salons were also meeting places where a well-titled but down-and-out nobleman might meet a rich bourgeois woman willing to be down-and-under his thumb.

Enlightened Moms

Many women identified with the ideas of Romantic love, popularized in the new novels, where the virtuous woman triumphs over evil (e.g. a lecherous boss). They also liked the idea of "enlightened motherhood": that girls should be brought up as rational creatures, not in order to carve out a life for themselves, but because reasonable women would make better wives and mothers.

Early Scholar-Governess

In the 18th century, Elizebeth Elstob managed to acquire an education by living with her brother at Oxford. She knew eight languages fluently and published various works in translation. In 1715 she compiled the first Anglo-Saxon grammar, the *Rudiments of Grammar.* It became the standard work on the subject. But when her brother died, she lost access to academic life and her means of support. She became destitute, and, though one of the foremost scholars in the field of Anglo-Saxon language and literature, she spent the last 17 years of her life as a governess.

Smarter than Voltaire

Emilie du Chatelet was a partner in research with Voltaire until his jealousy at her accomplishments severed their relationship. She went beyond the mathematical physics of Sir Isaac Newton, and she provided a bridge for the later idea of the "conservation of energy," fundamental to all subsequent physics. When she died, her insights entered the scientific mainstream but no one credited her with her own ideas. They thought it preposterous that a woman would come up with such notions. She's finally been recognized by David Bodanis in *Passionate Minds: The Great Enlightenment Love Affair* (2006).

Women: Not To Be

Women's sexuality threatened men's autonomous experience of their individuality and the social order, according to Rousseau. How dare they! So men continued to fashion a bourgeois image of women that denied them passion and anger. Furthermore, they were not to engage in any dalliances. The wife's marital fidelity was essential to her husband's self-esteem, always in need of propping up. He, on the other hand, could indulge his sexual fantasies with "fallen" women who were capable of showing real human feelings.

The theme of the "anxious male" and the "pushover female" found its clearest example in the works of the popular writer, Jean-Jacques Rousseau. In the character of Sophie (*Emile*, 1762), Rousseau created a female model who was "made for man's delight." But Sophie, who's being educated by her boyfriend Emile, gets corrupted when she takes off for the gay life of Paris. She badly wounds Emile through her pursuit of pleasure, luxury and other lovers. This was male territory and, naturally, she ends up having to pay for her mistakes. If Rousseau had let her get away with it, women might have thought themselves to actually be human.

Rousseau: Not the Doting Father

Rousseau lived with a serving woman, Therese, on whom he depended emotionally, owning none himself (he turned over their four children to a foundling home). His anxiety about his individuality was present in all his writings and was echoed by his contemporaries (*Becoming Visible*, 2nd ed., 1987). His vision of the "individual" included a firm commitment to the subordination of women to men, largely as compensation for men's loss of authority over other men, which had been going on for a few hundred years by now. Rousseau set the standard for the docile bourgeois woman and the bourgeois, rapacious man, still popular today in dime-store novels.

Women are summed up in his novel as having the power to destroy men because of their ability to attract, while their weakness is to be easily taken-in and seduced by men.

Actresses and Whores Set the Standard

The new aesthetics and erotica of this era glamorized fine ladies into sex objects. They were trained to adopt a femininity that traditionally had been stigmatized as the prerogative of actresses and whores. Respectable ladies now made themselves up extravagantly with powder, paint, patches and puffs, designed to entice the male gaze.

The phrases "make-up" ("making faces" was colloquial for having sex) and "making a figure" convey the artifice of it all, as Roy Porter explains in *Flesh in the Age of Reason*. The natural face was invisible behind the painted one. Eighteenth century cosmetics were caked, elaborate and garish of hue (like stage make-up). Nature's face disappeared behind visors, wigs, jewels, masks, fans, lace and gauze meant to conceal age, wrinkles and pock marks, and to tantalize at the same time.

Does She or Doesn't She?

One problem for men: they could no longer tell a woman's innocence by her blush, the classic indicator. The woman who wore rouge ("blusher" today) wore an imitation blush which camouflaged lost innocence, hiding the bare-faced cheek of the shameless woman.

Watch that Perfume

Worse, women were trapping men through their noses. The English Parliament finally passed an act in 1770 to "protect men from perfumed women," for fear that scented "witchcraft" might lure unsuspecting men into marriage (*The Story of V*, Blackledge, 2004).

Women Capable of Identity

Mary Wollstonecraft established herself as in independent person of letters, a very un-womanly thing to do at that time. Wollstonecraft exemplified the enlightenment message of living up to one's individual capacity, which men espoused for themselves. She believed that women, if educated, could have an *actual identity as adults* and that they deserved to have inalienable rights, just as men did.

The "Person" of Woman "Idolized"

In her *Vindication of the Rights of Woman* (1792), Mary analyzed the plight of women. She claimed that women were idolized by men, respected only for their "sexual character." This admiration both cheapened and weakened them because Protestantism detested idolatry. In this conspiracy, men sought women for their physical charms and women colluded with them by their flirtatious behavior. Women's goal, as she saw it, was to get the best guy in the marriage market. In this game, Wollstonecraft asserts, "males devise the rules and hold all the trump cards."

The Frivolous Sex

Ms. Wollstonecraft criticized women for their emphasis on clothing and make-up which made them weak and dependent. Men in turn accused women of vanity because of their preoccupation with appearance. Mary believed that women rightly deserved the reputation of being the "frivolous sex."

To Conquer is All

This made-in-manland model of women exploited their chastity: they had to keep their virginity to remain whole, while men struggled to take it away, to "prove" themselves. Conquest was all-important to weak men, in order to dispel their insecurity. Women were reduced to sought-after game, pawns in a game of seduction, resistance and conquest. Wollstonecraft saw marriage as no better than legal prostitution.

Education the Key

Wollstonecraft didn't want women to have power over men, only over themselves. It's the uneducated and irrational women who gratify male wants. Women needed to control their minds before they could control their bodies. Mary exemplified the difficulty of such control in her own love-troubled life, attempting suicide twice. One of her two daughters likewise took her own life. The other, Mary Shelley, wrote *Frankenstein* and was the wife of the famous poet, Percy Bysshe Shelley.

Women and the French Revolution

Women played an important part in the fall of the Monarchy in 1789. They were active in the storming of the Bastille. Seven-thousand women marched from Paris to Versailles, to protest to the king about the bread shortage. They demanded that he return to Paris. The King did, with a moldy piece of bread stuffed in his mouth.

It was the sight of the marching women and children that stopped the National Guard from firing their muskets at them. The women were a key element in the overthrow of the Monarchy. They wanted to legitimate the rights they enjoyed while marching and fighting shoulder-to-shoulder with the men.

Women Should Stay Home

But once the Jacobin revolutionaries were in power, they banned women's clubs and societies, to keep women from meddling in political affairs. In May of 1795, women were ordered to remain in their homes; groups of five or more would be dispersed. In 1804, the Napoleonic Code reduced women's status to that of a dependent. It made it illegal for them to make contracts or to have bank accounts in their own name. The "People's Rights" were bad for women cause they weren't people yet.

Women in the Industrial Capitalist Economy

In the 18th century women were simply fighting for the *right to work*, not for equal pay or equal rights. The industrial economy reinforced the separate male and female spheres. In Britain, France and Germany, guidebooks extolled a woman's maternal and domestic activities. She was defined as weaker and more delicate. Home was seen as a sanctuary, a haven from the fierce competition and materialism of the marketplace where men had to compete. Most women accepted their subservient role.

But as some women tried to enter the workforce, critics wailed about the decline of the family, and they complained about mothers abandoning their homes and children. But in working-class families, the labor of the wife and kids was essential for economic survival. The middle-class women who preached against women workers were usually having the lectern held up, dusted and painted by working-class women, while maids scrubbed their floors at home.

Women in the Colonies

Prior to 1750, the primary definition of women was from theology: they were secondary. Though runner-up to men, they did have an equal shot at the after-life if they obeyed their masters—first their father, then their husband, then their son. Once ensconced on their little, after-life cloud, they'd be expected to continue floating around waiting on tables.

According to His Specs

Men delighted in describing their ideal woman, an ideal which a woman was then expected to emulate. The ideal woman existed for a gentleman's pleasure and display, a trophy. Everything about her turned on her ability to please her husband, according to his standards, which were always changing. Better read the gross fine print.

Female seminaries were set up to prepare women for their roles as wives and mothers. Some taught ladylike skills, others taught needlework and table manners. A few tried to educate them so that they could talk to their husbands. But their primary goals were: to help women attract a suitable husband, to be a credit to his success, and to keep a good house. After that, they could go to the movies.

Spinsters Not Wanted

The prejudice against spinsters caused young girls to begin thinking of marriage almost before they left the nursery, and to enter that state by the time they reached their teens. Twelve-year–old Alice Lee in Virginia protested her kinswoman's "retarding her success" in marriage. William Byrd declared in 1727 that the most "antique Virgin" he knew was his twenty year-old daughter (*Women's Life and Work in the Southern Colonies*, Spruill, 1972). He'd already married off his three-year-old.

In the Southern Colonies

One of the favorite topics for journalists was "Reflections on unhappy marriages—what went wrong?" Some of the reasons given for the degeneracy of the married state: female extravagance, their excessive fondness for dress and display, and their neglect of domestic duties. The "cure" from *Lady's Magazine* (1773):

(1) change your fashionable way of living

(2) do what your grandmother did: go to church and get re-acquainted with your house.

Unequal treatment for Crime

It was not unusual for women and men to receive different prison sentences. In a murder case that involved three people, two men and a woman, the two men were sentenced to be hanged, the woman was to be burned alive.

Unsuccessful Ducking

Grace, accused of witchcraft, was being tried a second time, this time by "ducking." Dropped into the water to see if she would float--the classic proof of innocence--she started swimming instead. This was not in the program and a second jury of women declared that she was "not like them nor no other woman that they knew of." Not knowing if she was guilty or not, they ordered her to be put in irons in the county jail for further trial. She's still waiting.

Chapter 13

Women in Europe

Poor women in the 19th century had to bring their babies to work with them. With brandy-soaked rags as opiates, the kids were kept sleepy and/or drugged. Women and girls in the British textile industry started at five or six years of age, first as assistants to their parents, then staying on at the factory during adolescence. They typically worked twelve to thirteen-hour days in unhealthy and unsafe conditions. They endured beatings if they were late for work, if they used the bathroom too frequently, or if they took too long.

Jeanne Bouvier worked at a silk factory when she was eleven years old, from five AM to eight PM. She wound thread on bobbins for the equivalent of two loaves of bread for a day's work. She then crocheted shawls at home into the night for extra money. Worse still were the young women in the coal mines of Scotland and Britain, who ended up with deformed spines, cramps, and lots of accidents after pulling coal-filled carts on all fours like beasts.

Just as before industrialism, women earned between one-third to one-half of what men earned throughout Britain and Europe. Employers used low wages as an excuse to pressure women to go back home where they belonged. Patriarchal authority demanded that women be dependent.

Nursing, teaching and clerking opened up jobs for women in the late 19th century, but it was still only "pin" money, good for pinning up her hem and little else. Again, employers saw women's first role as reproductive; economic production was secondary. In fact, women didn't belong in the marketplace. Except to shop.

Her Purse is His

Women could not own property. In 1857 a thief was charged with stealing a purse, "the property of Henry Fawcett," from Madame Millicent Fawcett. A man and woman were considered to be one person, *femme covert*. She was "covered" with his legal identity (*Becoming Visible*). Smothered with the rest.

First to Run

In 1849, Jeanne Deroin, a Parisian, was the first woman to run for public office under a democratic regime. She urged women to teach men how to transcend their quarrels, at home and in politics. She also said women had a duty to intercede in civic and political life, for the sake of the kids. She was arrested and imprisoned for trying to organize a joint association of men and women workers.

And in Russia

Agitation for women's emancipation led to a freeing of the serfs in 1848. The women saw the similarity of the serf's "slavery" and their own "kept" status at home. Their activities led to the overthrow of the Tsarist regime.

The New Woman at Century's End

In the 1890's "feminist" and "feminism" entered the vocabulary, and there was an explosion of feminist publications. Havelock Ellis attacked the institution of marriage, as did Friedrich Engels and Eleanor Marx. In Sweden Henrik Ibsen wrote "A Doll's House" (1871). In the play, Nora walks out on her husband and kids in order to "find herself." She's still looking.

The New Women as Anarchists

A backlash ensued. The "new women" were charged with pursuing a "masculine course of individualism." Proponents of women's equality were branded as egotistic. Opponents said that equality would lead to social and political anarchy. If women were equal to men, the sky would fall and God would have to start over.

A Third Sex—Threat to National Security

Opponents of women's rights talked of unmarried, independent women becoming a "third sex" (*Becoming Visible*). And, more serious yet, emancipated women threatened men's virility and therefore national security. If men didn't feel sufficiently propped up, how could they find the courage to fight for the homeland?

Choice For Women?

In the first half of the 19th century, Utopian Socialism dominated in the polls. It was championed by the artisans, the men who made shoes, clothes and pots, who longed for the good ole days of the household economy, wherein men provided a living for their wives and daughters who stayed at home and behaved. As Pierre Proudhon, one of its advocates stated in 1839,

"*Women must be housewives or harlots, there is no other choice.*"

Marx Supports Women

Utopian Socialism lost out to Marxist Socialism under the *First Internationale* (1864-1876). With the triumph of Marxism, support for women's rights was assured. Karl Marx was the first one to understand

and articulate women's liberation, connecting women's independence with her ability to earn wages in the industrial economy. Once she earned wages, she would be freed from the shackles of men. Women were to be part of the proletariat, the working-class that would overthrow capitalism. As Engels stated, within the family, he's the bourgeois, she's the proletariat.

Marriage was seen as a form of exclusive private property (Marx, 1844). It restricted women's ability to participate economically. Their dependence on men facilitated and increased their exploitation by capitalism. Thus their double oppression: by their husbands at home and by their employers at work. The home subsidized the factory. Women were a capitalized, capsized bargain.

A Plan to Free Women

First, women had to gain the right to vote. Then they could use that leverage to gain economic equality, and that would give them economic independence from men. A dream plan for women, a nightmare for men.

Bebel: Better than Marx

August Bebel, a follower of Marx, wrote *Women and Socialism* in 1891. It went through fifty editions and was translated into fifteen languages before World War I. This book had a great impact on working-class women. He advocated that women have the right to vote, to practice professions, to divorce and marry freely, to own property, to dress freely, and to have sexual satisfaction.

He went much further than radical feminists, calling "twaddle" the idea that women had a "natural calling" to raise families. He asserted that the domination of women by men was a result of history, not of biology. Conditions became customs, then became law, and soon it was "natural." Women ended up accepting their subordinate position as a matter of course, not considering the source.

In Germany and France

The German Socialist Democratic Party (SPD) was formed in 1875. At the SPD Congress in 1891, they declared a policy of universal suffrage and the abolition of laws that placed women at a disadvantage with men. It became one of the key texts of socialists everywhere. In France a split evolved between bourgeois and working-class feminists. The former advocated property rights, the latter (who didn't have any) wanted equality.

Chapter 14

Education in 19th Century America

After the Civil War, the idea that a *woman's mind was limited by her reproductive body* became popular. In fact it flew off the shelves of apothecaries; everybody bought it, women included. People thought it'd cure the social strife caused by the recent war.

Can Women Think?

In 1872 Dr. Clarke of Harvard, in a speech to a Boston Women's Club, said that women weren't meant for higher education. He claimed that women lacked the capacity to succeed in college (*Beyond Separate Spheres*, Rosenberg, 1982). A heated discussion followed during which Dr. Clarke learned a thing or two about women's capacity as they dismantled first his argument, then its vehicle.

The Womb Thinks Not

Dr. Clarke mouthed the idea of Herbert Spencer, the renowned English philosopher, that the body forms a closed-energy system. If a woman uses energy to think, especially if it's a deep thought, then she'd have less energy available for her womb-doings. It followed that the mental strain of college would adversely affect the development of young women's reproductive organs. If she got a PhD, her baby might develop DHP. Clearly a National Security Issue.

It Even Weighs Less

No wonder women couldn't think straight. The famed neurologist George Beard proclaimed that women's brains weighed less than men's because women hardly used them. And when they did, it was for trivial stuff: how tight to tie the corset, which feet to wear with which shoes, and how high the hat? No wonder it weighed one-tenth less than men's.

Education: Dangerous for Women

Women risked, according to Dr. Clarke, nervous collapse and even sterility, if they indulged in too much learning. He pointed out the case of Miss D. who had entered Vassar, the first college for women, at the age of fourteen. She left four years later, an invalid (*Beyond Separate Spheres*). Dr. Clarke considered whether to enroll his daughter in Kindergarten Tech.

Doctors, always on the vanguard of scientific knowledge, emphasized that the womb dominated a women's mental as well as physical life. The result: a weak, submissive, uncreative, emotional, intuitive and all-around inferior personality.

Critics took Dr. Clarke seriously, (even his mother believed him). He espoused solid beliefs of the time. Feminist critics respected his drivel. At Vassar, administrators didn't want to overtax the students—no late-night study binges. Physical exercise was restricted during the first two days of a girl's menstrual period. And they were to read slowly, lest the words crash through the womb walls.

Darwin: Not Women's Best Friend

Charles Darwin, a man's man, said that men had made progress over the centuries because they had faced life's difficulties, like attending mice-hunting conventions, while women fell behind, living the easy life of skinning bears. Women's brains simply didn't evolve while cooking soup in their cozy igloos. Dr. Clarke seized on this: women's undeveloped brain couldn't tolerate the stimulus of education. Ideas would be too hot for their minuscule brains.

Furthermore, Darwin explained that a man's mental functioning performed best at the highest intellectual levels, while women performed best at the lowest thinking levels. Men excelled at reason, the highest level; women performed best at the lower emotional and instinctual levels. This made women closer to animals than to men. And animals need to be tamed.

Race Suicide?

If education could destroy women's reproductive capacity, race suicide was on the horizon. Additionally the masculinization of women would weaken sexual division, society's most essential stabilizing force. Dr. Clarke called it a crime before God and humanity. He promptly yanked his daughter from kindergarten.

Coeducation Dangerous

The University of Chicago, which opened in 1892, had to admit women for financial reasons. The president, Dr. Harper, wanted separate facilities for men and women, but that was too costly. Coeducation proceeded, though they feared the students would abandon codes of conduct that governed civilized relations between the sexes.

College Women Fertile

Dr. Harper recruited Marion Talbot, a spinster at thirty-four, to be the new Dean of Women. She went on to prove that college women were just as fertile as non-college women (she didn't test herself). Dr. Clarke wondered about his earlier decision.

Men and Women: Not that Different

Helen Thompson, a declared agnostic at the age of twelve, carried on research at the University of Chicago concerning men's and women's differences. Her conclusion: that men and women at the University of Chicago resembled one another in their behavior more than scientists or popular writers thought possible. Her work prompted psychologists to question their hereditary assumptions. And her demonstration of the over-lapping of men's and women's performances undermined the belief that the female mind was a secondary sexual characteristic. Dr. Clarke re-enrolled his daughter back into Kindergarten Academy.

Can Women Write?

Women were not supposed to write. They didn't have the ability for it. Their hands were designed to hold knitting needles, not pencils. In the 18th century, Christiana Mariana von Ziegler was honored publicly yet savagely attacked for her writings. She published a book of poetry, wrote nine cantatas that Johan Sebastian Bach set to music, and wrote other essays. Yet she was attacked in poems that satirized her and mocked her for her uppity-ness.

High Price to Pay

Until the middle of the 19th century, it was rare to find a female writer who didn't have to pay for her intellectual productively with a distorted and unhappy life. Frances Wright, a Scotchwoman and social reformer, lectured and wrote in the 1820's and 30's in the United States. She formed a utopian community where she advocated sexual freedom and racial intermarriage. She was viciously slandered in the press and in the pulpit, especially the pulpit. To be a "Fanny Wrightist" was to be a deviant.

And Then There's Emily

Emily Dickinson (1830-1886) cultivated eccentricities so that she could carve out space and time to work and think. She always dressed in white, and mostly stayed in her room where she spoke to visitors and friends from behind a half-opened door. Accepted as a recluse and introvert, she was freed from social obligations, marriage expectations and domestic duties. She didn't have to wear a corset like every other woman, and her white clothes were always in fashion at her house.

Saved From the Religious Bug

Emily resisted mightily the religious revivals that were sweeping through the countryside like an out-of-control virus, sucking up the juices of her friends and family. She confronted the patriarchal God who had "turned his back on man," and made "writing" her god. And she lived to tell the tale.

Can Men Read?

Though Emily wrote over eighteen-hundred poems, few were published in her lifetime. She eventually stopped submitting any poems for publication because editors routinely made changes in her punctuation, adversely affecting the poems' meaning. They didn't understand them; they wanted her to write like they did. Illiterate men were bad for literate women.

CHAPTER 15

FASHION AND BEAUTY IN THE UNITED STATES

In the late 18th century, American periodicals were filled with attacks on the excesses of fashion. The new republic, with its democratic ideals, didn't allow for the frivolity of fashion. The idea was for people to wear simple garb, made at home, like the Quakers. This didn't last long. The French, who had helped Americans gain independence, wore fancy duds. And, when it came to fashion and culture, Americans looked to Paris

Women Desire the "Latest"

Young women began increasingly to see themselves as different from their mothers. They no longer wanted to spin their own clothes at home. Suddenly, they wanted to be "ladies." They wanted the latest clothes, the latest furniture, the latest recipes, and plasma TV's.

By the 1830's attention was paid to fashion by women throughout the land. "Fashionables" were found in rural areas, even in log cabins of the back-country in Pennsylvania. Poorer people still made clothes in their homes, but they'd bring these to market to sell, then use the proceeds to buy the latest knock-offs from Paris.

The Corseted Waist

In China they bound the foot; in the Western world they bound the waist. Both were done for reasons of beauty. A small waist could be aided by dieting, but only a corset could hope to achieve an eighteen-inch waist, the stylish circumference from the 1820's on. Victorians believed that a woman's frail body required the support of a corset. "Tightlacing" was designed to accentuate the bust and the hips, and padding was in use by the 1830's to get the proper rounded form.

Like the clubbed foot in China, the tightly circled waist was symbolic of beauty and status. It spoke of paleness, fragility and bondage. The husband, boasting that he could encircle her waist with his outstretched fingers, demonstrated dominion over his domain. If his fingers couldn't meet, she'd have to take in another inch, or he'd resort to the finger-stretcher. Guess which?

The pressure of the corset caused pain and distorted the internal organs and rib cage. One mother had her daughter's "stays" laced too tight; she died when her ribs grew into her liver. Anna Held, Florenz Ziegfeld's famous wife, was rumored to have had her lower ribs removed to achieve her hourglass figure.

The corset restricted women's movement, rendered them dependent, and made them submissive. In accounts of 19th century fires, women occasionally went up in flames. They were unable to run because of immobilizing corsets and skirts that were too full or too tight. In 1867, in an English women's magazine, an article stated that 3000 women had burned alive that year and 20,000 women suffered severe burns and injuries because they wore crinolines, a stiff wool and horsehair petticoat, especially flammable (*Am I Thin Enough Yet*, Hesse-Biber, 1996).

For both Chinese women and Western women, body image determined identity and the rewards one received. In both cultures the alternatives to marriage were grim, and the pressure to conform great. Families wanted the investment in their daughters to pay off with a handsome marriage. The chance that she might get sick or die was seen as a market risk. Women on the early stock exchange. Live stock.

The Ideal Beauty: Sickly

The American idea of beauty in this period was the opposite of robust or healthy-looking, which would've been considered vulgar. The American beauty was an ethereal creature, someone who disdained the physical body, didn't like eating, and, in her desire for delicacy, tried to look ill. Actually-ill people were copied as models of female attractiveness (*American Beauty*, Banner, 1983). Invalidism was a competitive sport: the worse your illnesses, the more operations you had, the higher your ranking. Women in intensive care were featured on beauty billboards. The beauty shoots conducted in the morgue went too far.

The tight-laced corset contributed to the maladies sweepstakes. Frequent headaches, fainting spells, spinal and uterine disorders were common illnesses that resulted from this flesh-crushing fashion. When Josephine DeMott, a bareback rider and star of the circus married wealthy John Robinson, she laced her corsets to eighteen inches and carefully cultivated the fine art of illness, imitating the women in her new circle of friends. She carried smelling salts to revive herself after fainting spells. Stairs were difficult for women; at the top of each landing was a fainting couch.

Description of the Ideal: a Malnourished Barbie Doll

This frail, sickly beauty has a tiny mouth that resembles a beestung cupid bow or a rosebud. Her short, slight body has a small waist between a rounded bosom and a bell-shaped lower torso, covered by voluminous clothing. Small hands, tapering fingers and tiny, delicate feet (if seen) round out this early diminutive Barbie.

The Famous "Beestung" Mouth

Short of getting stung, which many women undoubtedly tried, there were instructions for shaping the mouth into the proper "beestung" shape. She was to repeat, in sequence, a series of words beginning with "p," which would round and pucker the mouth. Most popular were "prunes, peas and prisms." A 1913 etiquette manual advised a "belle" to enter a room with "prism" fading from her lips (*American Beauty*). In posing for the camera, the "beestung" mouth would say "peas" instead of "cheese."

Elisabeth Stanton, the women's rights' advocate, refused to hand out literature to women with "prunes and prisms" expressions on their faces, handing them bouquets of prunes instead.

Honest Beauty

There were attempts to counter the trend toward manufactured or artificial beauty. In 1827 the Murray sisters wrote *The Toilet*, a popular book of riddles that made the point: the true path to beauty is through virtuous living; self-control and sexual purity are essential to beauty. *Godey's Lady's Book* also advocated "moral cosmetics" in tales of drab appearances transformed by plain soap and clean living. One New Jersey woman accidentally ate a cake of ivory soap and became Miss America.

The Duty of Beauty

The idea that beauty was simultaneously *woman's duty*, as well as her desire, was being instilled into women's consciousness. First achieved by clean living, later by cosmetics, and eventually, when all else failed, by surgery.

The 1830's and 40's

Fashion accelerated its pace. Foreign observers claimed that American women followed the "fashion mode" more than women of any other country. Commentators referred to it as a mania, an obsession. Fashion was called a tyrant, a fickle goddess. It made women "old" by thirty-five. They donned caps, tucked their hair underneath, and had their teeth pulled. By contrast, women in France were peaking at forty, just like men in the U.S.A.

New and Better Products

Capitalism motivated producers to create new needs and to exploit new markets, most of them centered on the body and its functions. Advertising promoted insecurity and encouraged women to adopt critical attitudes toward their bodies, their selves, and their style of life. They rushed to buy the latest products (in order to be a good wife), and beauty products (to be cute and keep her man). The body was seen as an object that women could control and profit from.

Women spent a great percentage of their earned money to be "in fashion." In 1843, women in Philadelphia earned less for seventy-eight hours of work a week than a journeyman earned in a ten-hour day. Yet they tried to keep up with the latest in *Godey's Lady's Book*, the fashion magazine of the day.

Mutton Sleeves and Street Sweepers

The huge leg-of-mutton sleeves became popular in the 1830's. They were so large that women had to enter and exit doors sideways. The skirts of genteel women continued to sweep the streets, raising the hackles of street sweepers. Only prostitutes bared their ankles to excite passersby. And crinolines, introduced in 1842 to lessen the number of petticoats worn, were simply added to the rest, so a woman became a "sea of petticoats." Some guys drowned before they reached shore.

What This Town Needs

Is a good department store. Before Stewart's Department Store opened in New Your City in 1842, small specialty shops served the needs of women. One store on Chatham Street sold combs only, roosters in back. At Stewarts's, the "marble palace," a woman could buy everything she needed to outfit herself. As a "dry goods" store, there was no barrel of whiskey to slake your thirst nor a spittoon for men. But it did have fixed prices. And Mr. Stewart, like everyone else, advertised. His horses ate brand-name hay and their manure emerged with colorful tagged ads.

Arsenic Complexions

How did the frail beauty get that wan complexion? Before the Civil War, women were not supposed to use paint. Instead, they ate vinegar, chalk and arsenic to get that "delicate" look. It was rumored that the Circassians, the renowned beauties of the world living in the far-off Caucasus, ate arsenic to keep their beautiful looks. Arsenic stocks shot up, shelves were emptied, and women wobbled around looking whiter and whiter after downing the poison.

Dancing Fanny

Burlesque troupes with chorus girls were quite popular in these years. Fanny Elssler, a spectacular performer, made a rousing appearance in the 1840's. She had a fiery, sensual dance with staccato-like steps. When she was in town, the Senate and House of Representatives cancelled their sessions in order to attend her performance. The president wanted to make her Ambassador to the White House.

The 1850's and 60's

By 1850 people were wearing their "Sunday best" to church, the original fashion runway. They were able to parade their finery down the aisle at communion time. Easter was a special fashion date, with a longer show. As women slowly shuffled to the railing, hosts were held in abeyance and foot traffic was backed up suitably so that everyone could get a good gander.

Mannequins Win Labor Battle

The use of mannequins began around this time. Some stores still used live models to display clothes in the windows. In a contract dispute, the live models lost to the mannequins.

Words at Work

By the mid-nineteenth century, clothes took on symbolic meaning. A dress meant femininity, whether for domestic or frivolous use. If women were to do work (housework didn't count cause guys didn't do it), they needed to wear masculine clothes, since "work" was deemed "masculine."

New words came into use to describe the latest fashions: "elegant" in 1845; "stunning" in 1849, and "chic" in 1856. To save oil in greasing the thought-gears, these words were later recycled.

Hoop-De-Do

Hoop skirts were big in the mid-1860's. Women liked the freedom of movement; men liked the movement. As a woman swished and swayed, bits of undergarments were revealed, titillating for the Victorian sensibility. Women competed against each other, trying to outdo each other in skirt size. It became hard to get through doors or to sit on chairs. Forget elevators and phone booths. A plant manager at a window shades factory had to fire all his female employees cause their skirts kept brushing up against the shades. Husbands liked the hoop cause they saw the hoop five minutes before she arrived.

In 1867 the hoop was out. The clinging dress with the big, ever-changing bustle was in. The "Grecian Bend" or the "S-curve" arrived in 1868. It involved a tight corset and high heels, so that the bosom and buttocks protruded substantially. A Woman wearing it could not sit upright while riding in a carriage. She had to lean forward and place her hands on cushions that rested on the floor of the carriage. To read, the book had to be tied to her face.

Bloomers In-And-Out

Feminists kept trying to introduce dress reform, to give women looser clothes that would be healthier. One example was the "bloomer," a loose divided skirt, generally worn over pants. It gave freedom of movement to women and was modest, not erotic. No more debilitating corsets and good-bye to twelve pounds of heavy long skirts and petticoats. But there was a storm of protest in the U.S. and Europe. It became a comic icon of the women's rights movement. "Bloomer girls" were pictured smoking cigars and being waited-on by hen-pecked husbands. Preachers quoted the *Book of Deuteronomy;* it specified that men-only are to wear pants. Finally, it was rumored that prostitutes wore a costume resembling bloomers. The bloom was off.

Brains or beauty

Feminists were linked to bookishness and being intellectual; that meant they couldn't be beautiful. They were required to wear bluestockings to identify themselves as rebels who read. And their books had to have blue book covers to match their stockings.

Hooker Row

During the war, General Hooker provided the name for the brothel-lined street in Washington, D.C., also called Lafayette Street. Washington had over five-hundred bawdy houses during the war. Chicago had over five-hundred in 1860, and, in the 1850's, there was one for every sixty-four men in New York City. Lest we forget, the "Yellow Rose of Texas" was sung for the anonymous mulatto Madame from Galveston. All this in the interest of saving the virtue of the stay-at-home mom for whom sex was too yucky.

Cosmetics In

The prohibition against using cosmetics ended in the 1860's. Fashionable women now creamed and powdered their faces. They also used rouge, lipstick, and mascara. Enameling was back in vogue: women coated their face and neck with plastic enamel, a concoction built around an arsenic or lead base, for a smooth, light complexion. Women who used these dangerous lead-based whitening lotions, like Bloom of Youth, began to appear in medical case records after the Civil War.

Say "Peas"

The use of photography made appearance more problematic. Women who ordinarily shunned paint, requested it at photo studios. "Making faces" for the "public gaze" required makeup, just as it did for dancers and actresses. The use of makeup was crossing over from the stage to everyday-life through photography.

The 70's and 80's: Bustle In, Bell Out

The bell-shaped skirt was tossed out on December 31, 1869, and the tight-fitting dress with the still-changing bustle in the rear was "in" on the following morning. Feminist critics who didn't like the eroticism of the bell-shaped dress, which provided teasing glimpses of undergarments and flesh, hated this new wrinkle in fashion even more. It was difficult to move about in, and it was hard to keep up with the swaying, ever-changing bustle. To know what was "in," New York City dressmakers started having a fall and spring "opening day," when they would preview the latest bustles. The bustle was listed on the Stock Exchange where men could track its movements.

Cosmetics' Short Life Span

Cosmetics, which were okay in the 1860's, were now socially banned in the mid-70's because of their association with prostitutes. Enameling studios, formerly ubiquitous, were not to be found, though large drug stores employed assistants who could paint out black-eyes for men. Manicuring appeared at this time, one area in which women dominated, since men holding women's hands was too sexual an idea for men to contemplate. And women continued to give men black-eyes anyway.

Where are All the Men?

It was believed that husbands were difficult to find in this period, so women desperately worked on their appearance as a means of sexual attraction. With cosmetics off limits, hair took over.

Hair Craze

The British Blondes, a burlesque troupe that invaded the U.S. around 1870, inspired a craze for peroxide blonde hair and the use of false hair. False hair was needed for the intricate arrangement of the masses of hair displayed atop her head. Hairdressers were now needed for these labor-intensive productions. Advertisers claimed that the curls and waves on the front half of the head were the key to social success. *American Hairdressers Magazine* was started in 1878, and in 1888 the Hair Dealers' Association of the United States began issuing fashion statements to hairdressers (*American Beauty*).

McCall's Magazine in 1878 stated that hairdressers had complete control over fashion styles, and that they kept the voluminous and costly styles in vogue. Department stores introduced hairdressing salons by expanding the ladies' parlors. The fix was in.

Students Study Hair at Ohio University

At Ohio Wesleyan, officials tried to ban false hair because the students spent so much time fixated on their hair instead of their studies. One student took time out from her hair-fixing to state, "No woman under ninety-five is free from hair vanity." And she had a master's degree in Hairology.

Peel That Face

Face peeling or skinning was started in 1886. Acid and electricity were applied to remove the upper layers of the skin in order to give the woman a youthful appearance. As actresses reached middle age, they underwent face skinning. Later still, they skinned their knees.

Plump Up that Body

Now plumpness was suddenly in vogue. Scragginess was no longer lovely. Women scrounged around to find food they'd hidden away, weeks or months before, hoping this day would come. Women ate with a vengeance, watching the scale go up hourly. Medical authorities said that fat promoted health. Voluptuousness was good. Hotel bars displayed voluptuous nudes. Women wore the "gay deceiver" to parties; when it popped, she was embarrassed but the partygoers had a good laugh. The Germans, who had always held out against the thin craze, basked in their beer and potato salad. Life was gay.

The Gay Nineties

The pursuit of beauty, as women's role, took off in the 1890's with the spawning of beauty contests and beauty pageants across the land. These public festivals reinforced the centrality of physical beauty in women's lives and made beauty into a matter of competition and elitism, the opposite of democratic cooperation. According to *Harper's Bazaar* (1893), "the culture of beauty has skyrocketed during the past few years." Another change came with electric lighting, never popular with women, which made rouge necessary at night. Women had gotten so used to being in the dark that they preferred it.

Queen for a Day

Mardi Gras had long crowned a queen. The Tournament of Roses in 1889 began to crown a queen for the Rose Day Parade. In 1898 the Elks Club in several Ohio towns offered a prize to the township that sent the most attractive wagonload of women under eighteen-years-of-age. If they were over eighteen, they took them to the old folks home.

Voluptuous "In" (for now)

The British Blondes had foreshadowed the voluptuous woman of the 90's, someone who's energetic, emancipated, and erotic. The "S-curve" was still the favored flavor of this period. This shape resulted in a bosom that ran from the chin to the waist, achieved "naturally," by tightlacing. Chubby chorus girls were emulated, their waists laced so tight that the lines of their hips and bust distorted into balloon-like curves. Balloon makers threatened a patent battle.

Don't Exercise Those Curves Away

After women had taken up croquet, archery and tennis in the 1880's (still corseted and fully clothed), along came the Women's Christian Temperance Union. They advised against athletic pursuits for women because exercise "will destroy your voluptuous curves." The only athletic activity at Vassar was calisthenics, developed as a form of gymnastics-lite for women, and walking. Efforts to strengthen the body were seen as vulgar. Sweat was considered "indelicate." Some women attempted to eliminate their armpits, but were thwarted by attachments.

Fun at Coney Island

Working-class women made up for the lack of exercise by dancing. The *Ladies Home Journal* said of the "East Side Girl" in 1899, "She will work all day and dance all night." Working women frequented the dance hall during after-work hours seeking men to cavort with and pay the tab. At Coney Island it was customary for a woman to pick up a guy to pay for the evening, then take the trolley home with her girlfriend, not wanting to obligate herself to her date. If her girlfriend was gone, her partner might "exact tribute" for "standing treat." That would ramp up the evening's cost.

Hold That Dial

A few years later, the mood had changed from fat to thin, from heavy to athletic. Sarah Bernhardt, described as ugly (too thin) in earlier visits to the U.S., by 1900 was considered beautiful. Lillie Langtry from the U.K., likewise ugly previously (too athletic and too big a nose) became beautiful overnight, nose and all. By 1900, the voluptuous woman of the previous decades had gone back to the lower-class subculture.

The Gibson Girl

One of the new beauty models was named after the artist who drew her. She was tall, athletic, not quite voluptuous, but still big in the bosom and hips. She had a shock of upswept dark hair, with an emancipated look, ready to face the world. The new lithographic process idealized these images and they were easily mass-marketed. Men sported daguerreotypes of women in the brim of their hats. Pin-ups were everywhere. *The Police Gazette*, the *Playboy* of its day, flourished in barber shops, men keeping up on crime.

Trilby Conquers with Regular Feet

The other model that the public liked was the opposite of the Gibson Girl. Trilby, the heroine of George Du Maurier's novel of the same name, became an immediate sensation in the United States (*American Beauty*). Dozens of editions came out, people lined up to buy it. Amazon hired extra migrant workers, and Oprah featured it on her show. Public libraries had long waiting lists, and theatrical troupes toured the country with adaptations. Trilby hats, coats, collars, chocolates and Trilby III on the nearest screen. The fetish for small feet was now over because Trilby's feet were "neither big nor small," and regular-size mouths were now acceptable because she knew no "*p*" words and was allergic to bees.

Trilby does the Can-Can in 1894

Trilby was an orphan who lived in Paris with a rag picker and his wife. She made money by ironing clothes and modeling for artists. She smoked cigarettes, dressed like a man, posed in the nude with no sense of shame, and enjoyed the bohemian comradeship of the Latin Quarter. She not only delighted in dancing the can-can, but was promiscuous in her sexual relationships. (Conservatives threw up their hands trying to find a moral in this popular novel). Her love of a virtuous man made her feel guilty and led her into the clutches of the "devil," her music teacher, Svengali. The strictures of middle-class society kept Trilby's lover from her, and rendered him unable to love any other woman. Victorian propriety was thus trashed for what it was: all show, no glow.

Fashion Reform, Again

The dress reformers had been trying to make corsets looser, and were making some headway but the S-curve had detoured their efforts. The corset industry was very strong and tight-laced, and corsets had become more intricate, difficult to make at home. The fashion industry introduced seasonal changes to thwart the reformers' attempts at weakening fashion's manic hold. And the seasons kept getting shorter with weathermen blamed for colluding with fashion designers.

Daisy Miller Steps Out

In the mid-1890's, Daisy Miller, an exasperated young woman, tired at trailing dresses in the mud, wore an ankle-length skirt, three inches from the ground. Angry crowds followed her, shrieking with loud and derisive laughter.

The "Rainy Day Club," a group of dress reformers, decided to wear skirts that didn't trail in the mud. But if they wore these above-the-ground skirts on non-rainy days, they were met with whistles, catcalls, ripe fruit and vegetables. The Street-Sweepers Union decided to lower their pants out of solidarity.

Chapter 16

Women Have to Eat

Women were not comfortable around food. They were not supposed to be seen eating, which was a source of titillation for men. Eating implied digestion, defecation, as well as sex. These bodily indelicacies help to explain why constipation was part of the ideal of Victorian femininity. It was also a symptom of anorexia nervosa. Some women bragged that the "calls of nature" were but one or two per week.

Sensitive Stomachs

Dyspepsia, a form of chronic indigestion with discomfort after eating, was common in middle-class adults and their daughters. Caused by peculiar eating habits, the dyspeptic managed to live on a tiny amount of food. Sometimes heavy thoughts alone sufficed to stuff them.

Doctors stated that women were prone to gastric disorders because of the superior sensitivity of the female digestive system. A man's stomach was like a quartz-crushing machine that required coarse, solid food (*Fasting Girls*, Brumberg, 2000). A woman's stomach could be ruined by eating manly food. She needed foods that were soft, light and liquid. Jell-O, cotton candy and puffed-air were recommended.

Food and Ugliness

Abstemious eating was insurance against ugliness and loss of love. Over-eating robbed the eyes of their intensity and caused the lips to thicken and crack. Young girls learned that "the glutton's mouth may remind us of codfish--never of kisses." A woman with a rosebud mouth was expected to have an "ethereal appetite." The food industry sold pre-packaged cloud-bites.

Food and Spirituality

To be attuned to the higher senses--sight and hearing--a woman needed to neglect the lower ones, smell and taste. To admit hunger was not only a social *faux pas*, but showed lack of character. Denial gave you points. By refusing attractive foods you advanced in the moral hierarchy. A suppressed appetite and ill health sped you on to elevated womanhood.

Byron and Vinegar

Lord Byron was an early English cult figure who manicured, dieted by drinking vinegar, and was said to be disgusted at the sight of a woman eating. Women in Europe and the U.S. took up systematic fasting. Vinegar disappeared from store shelves.

Towards the end of the 19th century, a thin body symbolized status as well as spirituality. The frail woman was an object of beauty because she was unfit for either production or reproduction. An American advice writer, Marion Harland, called the "cultivation of fragility" a national curse. Body image trumped body function. According to Thorstein Veblen, in *The Theory of the Leisure Class*, a thin woman signified the idle idyll of the leisured classes.

Decrepit Women at Thirty

With their insides trashed by barbaric corsets, their bodies lacking nutrition and exercise, and their exteriors poisoned by creams and lotions, American women were wrecked by the age of thirty. Many commentators noted the striking contrast between the physiques of American and English women. "Premature physical decay," European observers called the loss of skin tone, sagging muscles and body deterioration that not even tightlacing could conceal. Some described then as "gaunt, sallow and scrawny." Catherine Beecher said that middle-class women were always ill, suffering gynecological ailments, emotional disorders and stomach problems. Beauty turned ugly for women.

Adolescents Join In

Adolescent girls simply imitated the behavioral styles of adult women. The bourgeois household was not adolescent-friendly for a girl. Confined to home, she may have had her own room but not the right to express her feelings and emotions. Having learned tact and reserve, her only "legal" outlet was to refuse food, quietly and politely. It was normal for a Victorian girl to develop a poor appetite and to skip her meals. (*Am I thin Enough Yet*?).

By eating minute amounts of food, the young woman could distance herself from sexuality, fecundity, and move up the social ladder. Plus she'd be sensitive, intelligent and moral besides. A healthy sickness.

Chlorosis, a type of anemia named for the greenish tinge of the skin, was popular among Victorian adolescent girls. Chlorotic girls avoided meat, lacked energy, and tended to lose weight as a result of poor eating. Doctors said that chlorosis was a phase they went through; it was accepted as a normal part of adolescent development. Non-chlorotic girls worried. Treatment was easy: large doses of iron salts and rest at home. Dr. Williams's marketed his "Pink Pills for Pale People," and patent medicines were freely prescribed. Chlorosis and dyspepsia shared weird eating habits with anorexia nervosa.

Romance-Driven

In the 1890's a fifteen-year old anorexic in a recuperative home, after being sent home "fat" after three months on a restrictive diet, disclosed to her keepers that her food refusal had resulted from her "passion" for a man who had admired another "extremely lean" woman. To win him, she walked excessively, starved herself, and laced herself tightly.

Moms Exert Pressure

The pressure to be thin, to appear genteel, came from mothers. Eva Williams, admitted to London Hospital in 1895 for treatment of anorexia nervosa, told friends that her mother complained about her weight. Her mom ran an ice-cream parlor and force-fed her ice cream on cream of wheat for breakfast.

Meat and Sex

Meat was the biggest problem for Victorian women and girls. The flesh of animals was thought to be heat-producing, leading to passion. Proper women, especially sexually maturing girls, made meat taboo. Adolescents were thought to be especially susceptible to meat. Doctors believed it stimulated sexual development and activity. Meat eating in excess was linked to insanity and to nymphomania (*Am I Thin Enough Yet*?). Therefore, by restricting meat-eating, one could moderate premature or rampant sexuality, as well as overabundant menstrual flow, not to mention hair loss, crooked toenails, and nightmares, and of coarse scuffed shoes

Strange food Fetishes

The clinical literature of the time mentioned foods that the adolescent girl craved: chalk, cinder, magnesia, slate pencils, plaster, charcoal, dirt, spiders and bugs (*Fasting Girls*). Rather than seeing her as iron-deficient, Victorian physicians assumed the adolescent girl was out-of-control, that the process of sexual maturation could lead to voracious and dangerous appetites.

Women Domesticated

Early in the 19th century, "home" became "women's sphere," the place of her enshrinement. The most revered feminine virtue was "enslavement" to the home. There was a small elite band of mothers and daughters in the urban northeast that set the agenda for the rest of the country. They defined women: what their morals should be, as well as their tastes, customs, and religious and political principles. They dictated the ideal to strive for, no matter how unrealistic it might be for most women, especially farmers.

The 19th century replacement for the earlier colonial working woman was now idleness or "gentility." The True Woman exemplified stability, piety, purity, submission and domesticity. Perfect for the True Man.

No Dirt Allowed

The functional character of household life was replaced with the ornamental attraction of the "Fair Lady" who shouldn't dirty her dainty hands with soil. Gardening was deemed unsuitable. Women were transformed from human beings into living objects of art, existing for the pleasure and pride of their husbands. Their beauty rested on their frailty, delicacy, purity, even their asexuality. Farmers' wives threw up their dirty hands.

Women became supervisors of a renewed domestic life, responsible for the quality of consumption and expanded childcare. There were new standards of cleanliness and a career-like responsibility to child-rearing. With the guy gone much of the time, the child took center stage, ready for the repressive atmosphere and sexualization that emblazoned Victorianism's marquee.

What about Laundry?

Laundering became a major component of housework in the 19th-century, according to diaries and letters of the times. This weekly, dreaded chore was very arduous, involving rubbing, wringing, toting, and ironing. When washable cotton replaced linen and wool, the amount of laundering multiplied. Women went looking for the boll weevil.

Word Police

The repressed Victorian household had to be careful what words came out. Better to say "light meat," rather than "breast;" offer her the "bosom," not the "leg." Don't use "woman" with its "womb" overtones; say "lady" or "female" instead. There was secrecy around pregnancy. It wasn't talked about, even between mothers and daughters. The gestation period was hidden until "confinement" came into play. A women wasn't pregnant; she was "with child," or she had a "woman's condition." And the stork, suitably diapered, made a convenient drop to wrap it all up. All in the interest of being "genteel."

Menstruation: Don't Mention It

Victorian moms thought if you said the word, it'd be forthcoming. Better not to broach it. One doctor estimated that twenty-five percent of girls had no idea what hit them. They thought they were wounded (*Body Project*, Brumberg, 1997).

To Be or Not To Be "Genteel"

Beautiful or not, every woman aspired to be "genteel." It was not "genteel" for mothers to wash or dress their children or to cook. To be a "good housewife" was very "ungenteel" (*American Beauty*). No exercise except for dancing. To sit in a rocking chair all day would be a day well-spent. A visitor to the U.S. in 1827 exclaimed: "Everything you do here is either 'genteel' or 'ungenteel;' you're victimized by inertia."

Can She Move

Feminine passivity was assured by her clothing. The weight and the number of garments severely restricted her movements. Public restrooms were out of the question. Getting in-an-out of carriages could take days. And if she fell, a crane had to be called.

Lower-Class Women Dealt Double Whammy

True Womanhood degraded lower-class women beyond their physical exploitation. Even a minor deviation, the way they walked, talked or wore their shoes, could put them outside the pale of respectability. Lower-class whites and Black women were recognized as necessary prey, there to preserve the most precious virtue of the Fair Lady. According to Victorian morality, if a woman lost her virginity, she was ruined, damned forever, unless she could get to a nunnery by midnight. Virginity was a bad invention for women.

African-American Women: A Different Sphere

If women occupied a "separate sphere," African-American women lived in the basement of that sphere, safely partitioned-off by a trapdoor from the rest of the house. Within that sphere, if women were seen as a "shrine," Black women were seen by whites as sex receptacles, co-dependents in assuring their own debasement. To function as slave and receptacle, they had to be annulled as women, as human.

By legal definition, a slave could not be raped. Both law and social thought encouraged white men to assume sexual access to female slaves. Some plantation owners brought the female slave into the house to live, while his wife clenched her teeth in silence. The Black housekeeper endured a "second slavery" to her white female employer, whose own internalized debasement made her feel inferior herself (*Segregated Sisterhood*, Caraway, 1991).

Extreme Double Standard

James Henry Hammond, governor of South Carolina during the 1840's, had sex with his female slaves, common enough, but also with four teenage nieces. When his brother protested, it came to light, damaged his reputation, and temporarily estranged him from his wife. But he recovered, and went on to serve in the U.S senate. However the reputation of his nieces was irreparably ruined: they could never marry. He had blamed them for not keeping his hands from straying (*Intimate Matters*, D'Emilio and Freedman, 1988). "Blame the Victim," still popular today with helpless, hapless guys in search of a fix for damaged egos.

Black Woman Forced to Prove It

In 1858 a Black female abolitionist feminist was forced by a white minister to bare her breasts to prove she was not an imposter at a women's rights convention (*Segregated Sisterhood)*. The minister then claimed to be blind and needed further proof.

Divide and Conquer

Light and dark Black women were pitted against each other as part of the white man's strategy. This led to attempts to "pass" on the part of lighter-skinned Blacks, and to Black women's obsession with hair which became the "enemy."

Women's Rights and Black Women

The women's rights movement, under the leadership of feminists Susan B. Anthony and Elizabeth Cady Stanton, had aligned itself with the cause of their African-American sisters. That came to an abrupt end when the Black Suffrage Amendment, giving Black men the right to vote (three-fifths of each person at least), was enacted rather than that of Women's Suffrage. After that, the white suffragist movement became an elitist, bigoted instrument for the advancement of white class privilege. White suffragettes had abandoned their earlier egalitarian moral principle of universal human freedom.

The South Rules

In the 1890's, lynching and rigid "black codes" of segregation prevailed. Ideologies of "pure womanhood" existed simultaneously with eugenic theories of Black "bestiality." The "southern view" of race had become the American view. At a southern women's rights convention in 1894, Susan Anthony asked Frederick Douglas, the famed Black orator who had been part of the women's rights movement from the beginning, not to attend. She didn't want to offend their "sensibilities."

The Culture of Lynching

Ida Wells, a Black journalist from Memphis, exposed the truth behind lynching. The white men's "dialectics" entailed the dehumanization of Black men, the debasement of Black women, and the construction of white women as property. In an 1892 editorial of her Memphis paper, she stated: It wasn't the "lust" of Black men to "rape" white women which defined antebellum society, but the desire of white women to seduce Black men (*Segregated Sisterhood*).

Ms. Wells further pointed out how, in an effort to tighten control over both Black and white women, white men had constructed both a cult of lynching and a cult of chivalry as manifestations of patriarchal power.

And Rape

Ida Wells and other black women of the "anti-lynching campaign" had succeeded in demystifying the patriarchal manipulation of rape. She showed *rape to be a political issue* for the first time. Women's rights advocates had previously tied rape to drinking. Unfortunately, the Woman's Christian Temperance Union refused to align themselves with Ms. Well's cause. By balking at the denunciation of lynching, they doomed the effort to create a multiracial women's movement against violence. The WCTU was drunk on ideology, too temperate to be Christian.

Working Women and Women's Rights

By the 1830's factory girls were involved in trade-union protests. In the 1840's the Lowell Female Reform Association bought out the *Voice of Industry*. This trade paper voiced critiques of "True Womanhood." They rejected attributes of the "Ideal Woman" which prevented their participation and full remuneration in industry. Wages for women were three to four times lower than that of men in comparable jobs. They also disdained the notions of "feminine frailty and weakness, social purity, and the moral superiority of passivity."

Women Split

By mid-century a split had developed between unskilled industrial workers and women in the growing professions: nursing and teaching. A further split was the dichotomy between women working at home and those working outside the home. There was a stark contrast between colonial America when a woman who worked was accepted as normal, and the mid-nineteenth century, when a woman who worked was seen to be out of place and judged negatively by society.

The 19th century industrialization and urbanization led to a fragmentation of social relationships between the classes and between men and women. Women of wealth and stature did not identify with women less fortunate than themselves, whom they benefited from in the persons of maids and servants. Indeed, they looked with disdain on them, seeing them as members of a different species. Now where did they get that idea from?

Declaration of Independence

In 1848 women and men met at Seneca Falls, New York, to hammer out a "Declaration of Sentiments." It was approved by sixty-eight women and thirty-two men, one third of those present. It was a radical document prepared by Elisabeth Cady Stanton, calling for the complete emancipation of women. The men were able to sign with one hand tied behind their back.

Adultery and Abuse of Women

As in other areas, the double standard operated in the realm of adultery. Women were twice as likely as men to be accused of adultery, and twice as likely to be found guilty. In 1843, the Louisiana Supreme Court awarded custody to the husband of an adulterous wife even though he had physically abused her and murdered her lover.

Rule of Thumb

The rule stipulated that a man might not use a stick thicker than his thumb to beat his wife. In abuse cases, women who submitted to physical abuse were seen to be more virtuous than those who left their husbands. There was virtue in being victimized, as long as you kept your mouth shut. And sometimes the man made sure it stayed shut, insuring virtue all around.

Chapter 17

Problems of Womanhood

During the 18th and early 19th centuries, abortion of early pregnancy was legal under common law. It was illegal after quickening, usually the 4th month. "Abortion" referred only to the miscarriage of later pregnancies, after quickening.

Bring on the Menses

If a woman didn't have her menses, she'd take drugs to unblock the menses—to restore order in her body. Women had a basic right to their own bodily integrity, their monthly period. It was a domestic matter. Until the 1840's, women weren't censured by society for aborting a fetus before "quickening."

In the years 1800-1830, the abortion rate was one abortion per twenty-five to thirty births. By the 1850's, with the increased pressures of Industrialism and the desire for smaller families, it had increased to one abortion for every five or six births.

Less Kids

In the mid-18th century, the average rural woman would expect to face childbirth eight or nine times. By the early 19th century that number had dropped to six, and in some urban areas, four.

Unwanted Kids

In the late 1800's, attitudes towards "bastardy" changed. Whereas it had previously been a moral problem with economic overtones, it was now seen as an economic problem with moral overtones (soon to become a social problem, a barometer of what's wrong with society). Women talked of "women in trouble" as "unfortunates," victims of social and economic circumstances rather than as moral pariahs or bad people. Prostitutes, abandoned mistresses, and unmarried mothers were all included in this category

Organized religion had little interest in abortion until it entered the public, political arena in the late 1850's and early 1860's. Until the mid-nineteenth century, the Catholic Church implicitly accepted early abortion prior to "ensoulment." The vigorous attack on abortion after 1840 probably resulted from the prevalence of married women attempting it. The anti-abortion advocates had emphasized the opposite, its prevalence among the unmarried. After 1840, an act that earlier had been dealt with in biological terms was now seen ideologically.

Abortion and Pulling Teeth

An unmarried girl, scared of being pregnant, could ask the family doctor to treat her for "menstrual blockage." He would use the same procedures for this as he would for inducing an early abortion, possibly even pulling a tooth, as it was believed that any bleeding would have the same flushing effect upon the womb as menstrual bleeding did. Dentists complained to the tooth fairy.

The AMA Crusade

In 1857, the newly organized AMA (American Medical Association) initiated a crusade to make abortion illegal at every stage of pregnancy. The "regular doctors" were eager to win professional power, control medical practice, and restrict their competitors, the "irregulars" (homeopaths, midwives and non-professional doctors). For the specialists, whose interest in the female reproductive system raised questions about their sexual morality, the antiabortion campaign was a way to proclaim their high morality in contrast to their competitors, including their patients and ministers, many of whom favored abortion.

Reactionary Response to Double Standard Rollback

In their antiabortion campaign, doctors were reacting to women's attempts to be admitted into the regular medical profession. Advocates of women in medicine argued that women doctors would protect women from sexual violations. The "regular" doctors were also expressing male anger over the feminists' battle to make men conform to a single standard of sexual behavior. Men could never abide for themselves the same behavior standard they set for women.

Redefining Menses

Dr. Horatio Storer, leader of the medical campaign against abortion, compared abortion to prostitution. In an attempt to discredit "quickening," he said that many women "never quicken at all." His propaganda aimed to erase the distinction between earlier and later stages of pregnancy, thereby redefining the restoration of the menses. What had previously been a simple "restoration of the menses" was now abortion. Dr. Storer equated abortion with infanticide (*When Abortion Was a Crime,* Reagan, 1997*)*. When he blamed the stork for kidnapping, his mother had second thoughts.

Cashing in on Fear

The antiabortion campaign used gender, racial and class anxieties to push the criminalization forward. Women who'd been agitating for personal rights and political reform were being punished. The "regular doctors" gave to legislators a weapon that white, native-born male legislators could use against women of their own class: low birthrates.

Birthrates of Yankee classes were down, while it was up for Catholics and immigrants. Anti-abortionists used the hostility to these latter groups, as well as to Negroes, to fuel the campaign. They particularly wanted the anti-abortion law enforced among white protestant women, in order to increase this targeted population.

Laws Passed

Between 1860 and 1880, laws were passed to eliminate the common-law idea of quickening, and to prohibit abortion at any point in pregnancy. Physicians had won the criminalization of abortion and retained for themselves the right to induce abortion when they deemed it necessary. Doctors thus claimed the scientific authority to define life and death, and women now had to submit to doctors to find out what they already knew.

Winners and Losers

Physicians entered a new partnership with the State and won the power to set reproductive policy. Women lost what had been a common-law right. Their own perception of pregnancy had been stolen from them. The physicians' appeal to the fears of white, native-born, male elites about losing political power to Catholic immigrants and women had succeeded.

Wealthy Still Shirk "Duty"

By 1887 families of foreign-born women were still fifty-percent larger than those of native-born women. The government wanted the wealthy to bear their share and not to evade their "womanly" duties. The president of Harvard worried that they would not be "replacing their own." They put in place strictures to limit contraception and abortion. The Comstock Act made it against the law to mail supplies or even *information* about contraception or abortion.

But it backfired. The rich used available loopholes to obtain contraceptives and abortions from physicians. The poor, shut out of under-funded and closed clinics (and unable to afford doctors) had more babies than ever, though abortion was still attempted.

Gunpowder and Chicken Gizzards

In the late 19th-century women resorted to a repertoire of folk remedies for contraception, including the drinking of gunpowder and eating dried chicken gizzards. To induce abortion, Black women in Texas used indigo or a mixture of calomel and turpentine to "unfix" or miscarry. In the Midwest, women rubbed gunpowder on their breasts and drank tea made of rusty-nail water. It didn't occur to them (as far as we know), to rub gun powder on the male member responsible and light it. Unenlightened.

Sexual Repression

Nineteenth century repressive sexuality was one manifestation of the total work ethic that required suppression of all social values previously associated with leisure and enjoyment. Sex was thought of as dirty, base and vile, but gratification was okay for men. In the family, this "painful and humiliating ordeal" for wives was for procreation purposes only. In the period from 1865-1893, the Women's Christian Temperance Union helped to raise the age of consent for girls from ten to fourteen years-of-age in thirty-eight states.

Orgasm Not Necessary

From the early Greeks down to the 18th century, people believed that female orgasm was necessary for conception. Once they realized this wasn't true, feminine sexuality was seen in a new light, rather dimly. The Christian church, always suspicious of female pleasure, ramped up its attack on women and sex.

Irony of it All

While some male doctors claimed that women were essentially passionless creatures, incapable of feeling sexual pleasure (and considered deviant if they did), other doctors were charging women for orgasms provided to them on health grounds (*The Story of V*).

A Threat to Social Stability

Richard Von Krafft-Ebing said sexual pleasure wasn't okay for women, even in marital intercourse: "Women, properly educated and normal, have little sensual desire." He saw women's sexuality as a threat to social stability. Charles Taylor, writing in 1882, said women have less sexual feeling than men and lack sexual passion. According to him, three-fourths of women take no pleasure in the "act." By 1893 the appearance of the sexual side in the love of a young girl was deemed pathological, and *one-half of all women were thought to be not sexually excitable.*

Surgical Sex Control

The next logical step, now that women don't need or want sexual pleasure, was to take out the organ most responsible. In the second half of the 19th century, over a period of ten years, British surgeon Isaac Baker Brown performed clitorodectomies at his clinic, the "London Surgical Home for The Reception of Gentlewomen and Females of Respectability suffering from Curable Surgical Disorders." He sometimes finished the surgery before a young girl could finish reading where she was at.

Criteria Expanded

At first preventative, the criteria for clitorodectomy soon broadened. Dr. Brown had begun clitoris removal in 1859; by the 1860's he was removing labia as well. Soon he was operating on girls as young as ten, as well as idiots, epileptics, paralytics and women with eye problems.

Science sanctioned these excisions, reasoning that removing the clitoris could cure conditions as varied as incontinence, uterine bleeding, hysteria and mania brought on by masturbation. No quack, Dr.Brown was elected president of the Medical Society of London. Famous as he was, he had trouble finding dates.

The following year, Dr. Brown wrote a book promoting clitoral excision—*On the Curability of Certain Forms of Insanity, Epilepsy and Hysteria in Females.* His views were disseminated in the local organ, the *Church Times.* It published a favorable review of his book, which contained the suggestion that the procedure be recommended to "suitable" parishioners.

A Cure for Divorce

Dr. Brown operated on five women who wanted divorces, each time returning the "cured" wife to the husband. "The mutilation, sedation and psychological intimidation seemed to have been an efficient, if brutal, form of reprogramming," according to a contemporary source.

In 1879 a twenty-one year old single woman had her clitoris and labia cut off at Chelsea Hospital in London to cure herself of irregular menstruation. And a nineteen year old had her clitoris removed simply because she was unmarried. The husbands continued on mistressing.

The cutting of the clitoris was seen as one way to stop women from masturbating. In the United States, J.H. Kellogg (of the Cornflakes Kingdom) proposed, over a bowl of wholesome cornflakes and milk, that pure carbolic acid be poured onto the clitoris, if girls didn't stop pleasuring themselves (*The Story of V*).

Ovaries Too

Ovaries also came under the scalpel. In 1855 over two-hundred ovariotomy operations were performed in the United Kingdom, with a death rate approaching fifty percent. Conditions for removing them included "masturbation, erotic tendencies, troublesomeness, simple cussedness and eating like a ploughman." The U.S., France and Germany also performed "*die castration der frauen*." The craze for female genital mutilation under the banner of "necessary medical surgery" led one doctor to write in a British journal in 1886, "Soon it'll be rare to meet with a woman whose sexual organs are entire" (*The Story of V*).

Ovaries on a Platter

Victorian doctors boasted about the number of ovariotomies they had performed, and they displayed the ovaries, arranged on silver platters, to admiring audiences at meetings of the American Gynecological Society.

Don't Pollute

By 1906, 150,000 American women were without ovaries. It had become a social judgment to prevent the "unfit" from breeding and polluting the body politic. "Unfit" could be any woman corrupted by masturbation, contraception, or abortion. From the 1890's to World War II, mentally ill women were castrated. Mentally ill men were given extra testosterone.

Orgasm Not Desirable

Physicians and popular culture, including some feminists, tried to make women-without-orgasm the norm. They shouldn't even want one! Desire is not desirable. The old wisdom that sexual gratification was necessary for health was now in conflict with the intrinsic "purity of womanhood." The solution was to promote the idea that women desire maternity, not sexual orgasm. This was to protect the fragile male ego, always on the verge of collapse, from thinking it had anything to do with a women's pleasure.

Women: Sick of Being Sick

In the 19th century the pathology of women's sex was extended to nearly every aspect of her physical being. Catherine Beecher stated in 1855 that women of her time were sick simply "because they were women." The ailments: pelvic disorders, sick headaches, general nervousness—all were seen as symptoms of "female complaints," nervous disorders thought to be linked with the malfunctioning of the feminine sexual organs.

Albert Hayes, writing about hysteria, chlorosis and nymphomania in 1869, was one of many medical authors of the day who saw the female reproductive tract "as a veritable swamp, rife with pathogenic miasmas." The power of the reproductive force, when awry, spreads confusion and disorder throughout the body where it rages capriciously. After saying that he collapsed.

What Causes It?

A French physician Pierre Briquet said hysteria was caused by the bad treatment of the husband. He claimed that one-fourth of all women suffered from this disorder. On the other hand, William Griesinger, another 19th century physician from America, argued that hysteria cannot be caused by sexual frustration because of its great frequency among married women." Dr. Giesinger did not study logic.

A Godsend, in any Case

Doctor Trall saw hysteria in women as an economic godsend to medicine. In the late 19th century he estimated that three-fourths of the female population was "out of health," and that this group constituted America's single largest market for therapeutic devices (*The Story of V*). Of the $200 million earned by U.S. physicians in 1873, he estimated that three-fourths of that, "our physicians must thank women for." Seventy-five per-cent of his own practice was devoted to treating diseases peculiar to women.

Male Doctors Make the Rounds

If the normal functioning of female sexuality was defined as a disease, women must indeed be frail. During the decade that Dr. Trall wrote this, the proceeds of treating women would have equaled almost one-half of the entire federal budget. Charles Bigelow, writing in 1875, discussed women patients who were dissatisfied with their marital sex lives:

> *Almost every physician of a large practice has a circle of "everlasting patients" whom he visits and prescribes for once a week, on the average, for years.*

The Solution to Women's Problem

Bernard Mandeville prescribed horseback riding for hysteria in young girls combined with a regimen of massage for up to three hours daily. The 1899 edition of the reference guide for physicians, the *Merck Manual* recommended massage as a treatment for hysteria. Elsewhere, it suggested sulphuric acid as a remedy for nymphomania. Ouch!

Mr. Kellogg tried to market "Acid Flakes for Girls."

The Water Cure

Hydrotherapy or the "water cure" came to be the treatment of choice for women "suffering" from hysteria. The "cure" could be administered in a doctor's office, at home, or at fashion spas. Vast crowds flocked to Saratoga in the 1840's, many not even pretending to be afflicted, to get the "Saratoga Cure" or the hydriatic douche.

The fashion for hydrotherapies lasted more than fifty years in Europe, Britain and the United States with an emphasis on women patients. They were simply not afraid of the "water cure." It was safe, while over one-half of surgical patients died from the operating table. It began in the 1830's and 40's and continued in popularity till the end of the century. In Europe physicians handled the "operation" themselves. In the U.S. the medical profession was a bit squeamish, and doctors let a therapeutic assistant handle the "operation."

The Bumpy Cure

Railroad travel was also recommended for hystero-neurasthenic disorders. Dr. Jean-Martin Charcot, of the famous Salpetriere in France, sent some of his patients on long trips over rough trackbeds for their health. Then he and his colleagues realized that shaking their patients in place with vibrating helmets and jolting chairs would do the trick. In 1893 Charles Hartelius patented an electrical attachment for a rocking chair. The rocking motion sent an electrical current through the patient. The higher the voltage, the bigger the charge.

The Country Gets Wired

Electric lights were introduced in 1876, and women became significant consumers of electrical appliances. The first home appliance to be electrified was the sewing machine in 1889, followed by the fan, the teakettle, the toaster and the vibrator. The vacuum cleaner and electric iron followed.

Vibrotherapy

Vibrotherapy was advertised for ailments in men and women. "All nature pulsates and vibrates with life" (*The Technology of Orgasm*, Maines, 1999). Though invented in the late 1880's, vibrators didn't become popular until the early 20th century. Needless to say, men were threatened.

Summary

On the social level, Mary Wollstonecraft realized that men played the flirting game with a stacked deck and their sole desire was to deck the stacked woman. Economically, Marx and Engels fleshed out Women's double enslavement, at home and at the factory. But it took Babel to pop the Motherhood bubble, calling it "twaddle."

When women began to assert their individuality, men feared they were becoming a "third sex," a threat to their virility, as well as to national security. If women were to stand up, they'd have to stand down.

Men, fearful of women encroaching on their fiefdom, laid claim to women's body, throwing down the gauntlet to thwart their march to human-hood. If women were actually human beings, what would men be?

Victorians used sexual repression to castrate women, literally and figuratively. It was a way to "take away" her "problems." If she wanted a divorce, she could be "cured" by castration. For young girls, carbolic acid was recommended if they were too frisky. On the other, far side of the coin, it was nothing short of hysterical, the way doctors made huge sums of money off of women's "problem" of hysteria.

QUIZ #4

1. Bourgeois women were supposed to:
   a. filter out industrial grime with their multi-layered petticoats
   b. provide a soft pillow for their hard-headed taskmasters
   c. accept their Alice-in-Wonderland status

2. Education was considered dangerous for women because:
   a. learning could cause the womb to re-locate
   b. facts would startle the tiny mind and rupture the thought-vessels
   c. if women started learning things...they might find out about men

3. Dr. Clarke decided to enroll his daughter in Kindergarten Tech. because:
   a. he knew she'd never graduate
   b. Kindergarten Academy would over-stretch her brain membranes
   c. education was cheaper than abortion

4. Women were not paid as much as men because:
   a. employers banked on keeping women's self-esteem at low interest
   b. the marketplace wanted women in the home at zero pay
   c. women's reasoning capacity didn't extend to money
   d. men's egos were too fragile to contemplate

5. The idea behind corsets was to:
   a. provide a healthy alternative to foot-binding
   b. provide a handy measuring device for a man's hands
   c. prove that nature provided too many ribs
   d. revitalize the smelling-salts industry

6. The "beestung" mouth was achieved by:
   a. setting up a bee colony in the boudoir
   b. saying "b words" while exhaling a bee
   c. chewing on a rosebud while inhaling the thorn

7. The whole point of women achieving beauty was:
    a. to make women's egos oscillate with the changing seasons
    b. to make women's bodies a commodities market, trading fats and curves
    c. to make women compete on an even playing field, themselves, not men

8. Fashions originated as:
    a. a way to increase church attendance on Easter Sunday
    b. a way to keep the streets clean
    c. a way to keep women busy and out of mischievous things, like thinking

9. Beauty pageants began as:
    a. an excuse to get women to parade in front of men
    b. an excuse to get women to parade half naked (in front of men)
    c. an excuse to get women to vie sexually for men's vile eyes

10. The "S-curve" body was popular because:
    a. women could ride in carriages without looking out the window
    b. it helped men remember what came before "t"
    c. it deteriorated women's health faster, making them more attractive

11. Eating meat was dangerous for women because:
    a. it could cause the hair to vibrate and fall out
    b. it could cause premature pregnancy, and possibly virgin birth
    c. women's digestive systems would over-heat, requiring anti-freeze

12. Women didn't want to be seen eating because:
    a. men might think they were human beings
    b. men thought that eating was like sex, and women liked it that way
    c. if they were eating meat, they might go crazy

13. Women were thought to be unhealthy because:
    a. they ate arsenic for breakfast
    b. they were scraggily, wind-blown, and looked 90 at 30
    c. they provided most of the income for doctors

14. Hysteria was caused by:
    a. married men looking the other way
    b. women who looked the wrong way
    c. too many petticoats

15. The Cult of True Womanhood required:
    a. women to disavow dirt and swear to sweep the streets
    b. women to take the pledge not to clean the house nor cook
    c. women to become asexual, thus promoting doctor's hysterical looting

PART FIVE

1900 TO 2007

CHAPTER 18

WOMEN STILL DO THE WORK

When electrification began, women were urged to buy appliances that would use the new "electricity." When they didn't buy enough appliances, housewives were urged to fire the servants, buy a sewing machine, and have more time for the kids and shopping. Especially shopping.

Women Work More, Earn Less, Own Nothing

World-wide, women represent one-half of the population, but perform two-thirds of all working hours, receive one-tenth of the world income and own less than one percent of world property. Of the 1.5 billion people living on less than $1 a day, seventy percent are female, with 96 million young women aged 15-22 unable to read or write—almost double the number for males ("Discrimination Against Girls 'Still Deeply Entrenched,'" Judd and Griffey, *The Independent,* May,2007). Throughout the west, housework generates from twenty-five to forty percent of GNP.

Eighty percent of all working women cluster around gender-segregated occupations in which wages are artificially low. Women make up two-thirds of all the minimum-wage workers in the U.S. And each year there are less mothers trying to "do it all," hold down a job while wrestling with kids and housework.

Women Do the Chores

Many women work part-time. Even when working full-time, they still do all, or nearly all, the unpaid work that they used to do. In the United States, partners of employed women do less work than partners of full-time homemakers. The working week of American women is twenty-one hours longer than that of men *(Beauty Myth, Naomi Wolf,* 1991) They do eighty to ninety percent of the chores related to the house. In Italy, eighty-five percent of mothers with children and full-time jobs are married to men who share no housework. Italian men believe that housework will infect them, make them impotent, and they will die.

Take Back the Appliances

In 1965 the average American woman spent fifty-four hours a week on housework, including kid-work. This amount is not that different from the time spent by affluent housewives in 1912, or for rural and urban housewives in 1935. Essentially, from 1920 to 1970, the amount of time spent on housework by non-employed housewives was constant throughout the period (*More Work for Mother*, Cowan, 1983). And they spent the same amount of time whether they had appliances or not. Shopping time shot up.

After WW II, housewives on farms spent sixty hours a week doing housework, while big-city wives spent eighty hours a week, wishing they'd stayed down on the farm. Clearly, life has gotten much better for women.

When It was Really Bad

Some of the most dangerous work that women did was in the sweat shops of the early 20th century. Susan began, at seven years-of-age, to work for the Triangle Shirtwaist Company in 1901. She worked from 7:30 AM to 9 PM for $1.50 per week. Little scissors were provided to cut thread off garments all day long. The work was monotonous, and they weren't allowed to sing. If a raid was to take place, the employers had the kids hide in large baskets. In 1911, a fire destroyed the factory. The fire escape had been locked, and 146 women perished. The owners were fined $75. They're still appealing the fine.

Servants Down, Tasks Up

As household assistants declined, fifty percent from 1900 to 1920, the number of household tasks increased. The housewife had fewer kids, but she was expected to do things her mother would never have dreamt of doing: preparing infant formulas, sterilizing bottles, weighing kids daily (after each meal), keeping them isolated at the slightest illness, consulting with their teachers, and chauffeuring them to dancing lessons and evening hip-hop parties.

These new tasks were not necessarily burdensome, but were time consuming and they required the acquisition of new skills. For example, the modern housewife didn't know how to shop. She had to be taught, not just to be a consumer, but to be an informed consumer. "Wise consumer practices" advised her to buy new things under the guise of training her in her role as skilled consumer, according to Ruth Rowan ("The 'Industrial Revolution' in the Home: Household Technology and Social Change in the 20th Century").

Bring on the Appliances

With fewer household servants, there was more demand for labor and time-saving devices. And, with more tasks to be done, there was a need for more specialized products. With more guilt at not being able to keep up with the increased burden of tasks and responsibilities, women were inclined to buy more and perpetuate the Industrial Revolution.

Advertising perpetuated the idealized image of the 1920's home: the woman who cheerfully and skillfully sets about making everyone in the family perfectly happy and perfectly healthy. She is neatly manicured and coiffured, her housework an expression of her personality and of her affection for the family.

This view of housework reflected a change. Prior to World War I, it had been a trial and a chore. After the war, according to Rowan ("Industrial Revolution in Home") it became an "expression of love" (laundering), a way of expressing "deep-seated emotion" (feeding the family), an example of "protective maternal instincts" (cleaning the bathroom), a way to "build the baby's sense of security" (diapering).

Emily Post added a new chapter in 1937, dealing with problems faced by "Mrs. Three-in-One"—the woman who had to be guest, waitress, and cook at her own dinner parties.

Lay on the Guilt

Guilty if the kid didn't gain weight, embarrassed if the drains got clogged, guilty if bathroom germs were not eradicated—the discovery of household germs prompted a fetish of cleanliness—guilty if the kids were unpopular at school because the clothes were old-fashioned.

In the previous century, mom felt guilty if she abandoned the kids; now all it took was her child going to school with scuffed shoes. Ads in the *Ladies Home Journal* between the wars used "guilt" as one of its top three appeals to women. The other two were "celebrity" and "social status" (*More Work for Mother).*

The Stove: less work for him, more for her

Labor-saving appliances backfired for women. The stove saved the male the task of cutting and fetching wood. But for the woman it meant the end of one-pot cooking and increased the amount of time women spent preparing meals. Diets also became more varied, entailing even more cooking.

"Water closets" replaced the chore of collecting "slop" buckets, but toilets had to be cleaned, a women's specialty. Home canning equipment made it possible to preserve fruit and vegetables, but vastly increased the seasonal amount of work a woman was expected to do. Candles, replaced by glass globes of oil and gas lamps, had to have the soot removed almost daily—another time-consuming chore for housewives. (Cowan, *More Work for Mother)*

Piped-in water meant woman had to "produce" clean toilets, bathrooms and sinks. Standards of excellence were raised. And with electrically powered washing machines, do-it-yourself laundry came into being. Bendix made it easier to launder, but now there were tons more to be done: sheets and underwear were changed more often, sometimes hourly instead of monthly.

With manufactured cloth, people were expected to own more clothes. There was a radical increase in the amount of sewing to be done. Keep in mind that there was no women's clothing in the Sears catalogue of 1894, but by 1920 there were ninety illustrated pages (*American Beauty*).

More Trips to the Store

Refrigerators made it possible to purchase foodstuffs in small quantities. This meant more trips to the market in the automobile. The auto accelerated the trend to dispense with delivery services formally provided by retailers. The auto not only replaced the horse and buggy; it also replaced the iron stove as the locale where the housewife spent her time and energy.

Too Much Drive

By mid-century, the time that housewives spent driving to stores, shopping and waiting in line (instead of preserving strawberries and stitching petticoats), used up whatever time they saved. Instead of bedside care for the sick, now they had to drive feverish children to the doctor or hospital. Or to the train to pick up relatives, or to a baseball game. Or around the block to escape the cluttered, appliance-filled kitchen.

CHAPTER 19

VIOLENCE TO WOMEN

It's fairly common. Twenty-five percent of the violent crime in the U.S. is wife assault. Four million women in the U.S. are victims of domestic violence each year. One-fourth to one-half of women could expect to experience domestic violence at some point in their lives, while fifty-per-cent of all married women suffer physical abuse from their husbands at least once in their marriage. One-third of all calls for police assistance in the U.S. concern domestic violence. And this is on a quiet day.

In Sweden there was a seventy percent increase of reports of violence against women between 1981 and 1988. Worldwide, violence against women is the most common crime. According to Cesar Chelala, forty-two percent of women in Kenya and forty-one percent in Uganda reported having been beaten by their partners ("Changing Cultures to Value Women," *Philadelphia Inquirer*, 4.29.07). In India, law-enforcement officials often ignore women's reports of violence. According to the Mexican Health Ministry, about one in three women suffer from domestic violence, and about 6,000 women a year die from it. Rape and beatings usually precede the murder of women ("Changing Cultures to Value Women").

"If Only I Could Be Better"

Children often blame themselves for violence in the home, whether directed against them or their mother. Besides guilt, kids also suffer side effects from their mothers. The violence directed towards mothers makes them "afraid and bitter and hateful towards their sons, and jealous and overly protective and angry at their daughters" (*Insecure At Last*,Eve Ensler, 2006).

Equal Opportunity Victims

Often thought of as a lower-class activity, beating is also practiced among the upper class, though it's most popular among the middle class. In *Not to People Like Us*, Susan Weitzman explores the subject among couples earning $100,000 to 500,000 a year. The spouses of these couples had post-graduate education, and many had successful careers as well.

Susan (not the author) was one example. At various times in their 20-year marriage, Rod had dragged her by the hair, thrown furniture at her, choked her to within moments of her life, banged her head against the walls and floor, and punched her. A few months before their divorce he had broken her jaw, permanently disfiguring her beautiful face. She also had permanent hearing damage as a result of her husband's screaming rages: after he'd thrown her on the floor, he'd scream obscenities directly into her ear, part of her "punishment" when he was displeased with her.

The richer the abuser, the more they feel above the law. With the means to hire the best lawyers, they often are (e.g. O.J. Simpson). More than half of the women in the study reported fearing for their lives. The other almost-half were nowhere to be found.

A Brief Beating History

Wife beating was "the single most common cause of family violence in the colonial Plymouth courts." Those courts still "placed family preservation ahead of physical protection of victims." Wives had fewer rights than slaves who could refuse their masters the "final familiarity."

Wife-Beating Normal

In the early part of the 20th century, women were more concerned with their husbands bringing home the bacon than they were of getting beat. It wasn't till improved social conditions upped their aspirations and expectations that it became a concern (*Heroes of Their Own Lives*, Viking, 1988). In 1910, a mother who was permanently crippled by her husband's beatings complained only about his failure to provide. In 1917, an Italian-born husband had battered his wife for years. As explained by Linda Gordon in *Heroes of Their Lives*, he ended the relationship by forcibly committing her to a mental hospital, despite attempts by the thirteen-year-old daughter to convince the caseworker that physical abuse was her main problem.

Keep the Family Together (whatever the cost)

After World War I, if there were family problems, the social workers' goal was to return the family back to "normal," to the status quo. The idea was to keep the "castle" private. If they had to intervene, they sought to educate women to be better wives. The focus was on the victim: she was the one needing fixing, not the batterer.

This meant the maintenance of marriages that were brutal prisons for women. Couples were told that neither was to blame, but the wife was identified as the "client." She was more agreeable and more malleable. After a court hearing, the judge would typically tell the wife to "be attractive and keep a nice house."

Through the 1930's, the focus was still on non-support, not physical abuse. A shift occurred in the 1940's: though women still blamed themselves for being beat, they now wondered if it was such a good idea (*Heroes of Their Own Lives*).

Freud Dreamt of Passive Women

After WW II, Freud championed the idea of the "passivity of women." According to this theory, if a woman wasn't passive (the polarities again), she suffered from a masculinity complex. That made her incapable of fulfilling her role as wife, child-bearer, and mother. To top it off, in their penis-deficient state, women envied men and couldn't think of anything better than marrying "dear ole dad."

Deutsch's Turn for the Worse

Helen Deutsch, a disciple of Freud, developed a theory of masochism that applied to girls who were beaten or raped. According to her strange logic, women who were raped by men were expressing their unconscious desire to be raped by their own fathers. In their masochism, these women desired a symbolic father, as represented by another man, to rape them. Helen's father claimed he didn't know her.

Worst for Women

This became the dominant psychiatric explanation of why women became victims of domestic violence, and why abused women stayed with the perpetrator. It was all their fault: they were choosing it. Because of their biology, because they were women. Psychiatrists believed that such women secretly enjoyed the pain inflicted on them, and that these women actually sought out men who would mistreat them. This is still sold at your local drugstore.

Before the 1970's, sex-role stereotyping, sexism, and cultural acceptance of violence as a form of discipline—all of these contributed to the abused woman's feeling of being trapped. Women were expected to fulfill their roles as wives and mothers; men were granted the privilege of ruling his castle. Women, dependent on their husband for financial support, were forced to tolerate whatever tyrannies he might mete out (*Not to People Like Us,* Weitzman, Basic Books, 2000).

Nothing New

Violence and aggression toward women were glamorized in the movies and on T.V. in earlier decades. The norm was cruelty. In the 1950's sit-com *The Homeymooners*, Ralph would often say, shaking an angry fist toward Alice, "One of these days I'm going to bop you in the kisser." James Cagney, in the 30's, opined that every now and then, "A dame needs a grapefruit in the face to keep her in line."

Rape: Another Form of Violence

In patriarchal societies, rape was understood as a crime against family property, having nothing to do with the woman involved. Women have evolved. Instead of being a piece of property in the old days, today they're a piece of meat. Still not a person in their own right. Rape was previously seen as a crime motivated by sexual desire. Feminists redefined it as a crime of power, enacted by men to control women. Doctors agree: in *Obstetrics and Gynecology* (a medical schools' textbook), the normal act of intercourse was said to contain "an element of rape."

Susan Brownmiller expands on this in *Against Our Will: Men, Women, and Rape* (Ballantine, 1975), saying it's nothing more or less than a "conscious process of intimidation by which *all men* keep *all women* in a state of fear." Until her late thirties, Eve Ensler kept her "bedroom out in the open in the living room so no one could get me" (*Insecure At Last,* Villard, 2006*)*.

No longer his Castle

Though the women's rights movement in the middle of the last century exposed the problem of abusive husbands, it wasn't until the 1970's that feminist efforts had a mass impact. Rape was redefined to include attacks by acquaintances and husbands. New terms were coined: "marital rape," "date rape," "sexual harassment" and "domestic violence." The distinction was finally broken down between "public" and "private." Men's customary use of force within the family was rejected. His castle had been penetrated.

Juries Purposely Prejudiced

When the Women's rights movement began, juries in rape cases were still required to hear the 17th century dictum, "Rape is the easiest claim to make and the most difficult to prove." In North Carolina only virgins could claim rape. And since they weren't they were thrown out.

Rape as Normal

In our culture the depiction of sexual violence and rape has become so common that boys and girls think that rape is normal. A UCLA study showed that among younger adolescents, one-half thought it was okay for the guy to rape his girl if he was sexually aroused. A Toronto study showed that children learn dominance and submissive patterns at earlier ages. Sometimes in the womb.

Around the World

A 1983 survey of San Francisco women revealed that forty-four percent of them had survived rape or an attempted rape. In a Dutch study thirty-two percent of the women had experienced forced sex before the age of sixteen. There was a fifty percent increase of reported rape in Sweden between 1981 and 1988. In Canada one woman in four experienced her first sexual encounter under conditions of force.

Women to Blame

In *The Guardian Weekly* (December, 2005), an Amnesty International report revealed that one in three people believes that women who behave flirtatiously are at least partly responsible if thy are raped. A similar number think that women are partly or wholly responsible for being raped if they are drunk, and more than a quarter believe that women are responsible if they wear sexy or revealing clothing. The other three-quarters think women should don the burka and forget about it.

Convictions Rates Plummet

A study in 2002 found that one in twenty reports of rape led to conviction, compared with one in three in 1977 in the U.K. It's back to business as usual.

Freud Still Around

In Britain, a woman claimed that her physiotherapist raped her. The charge was denied; it was suggested that she had fantasized the rape and that such fantasies are common among women (*Intimate Matters*).

Serious Consequences

The most common reaction of rape survivors is a feeling of worthlessness, hatred of their bodies, often accompanied by eating disorders. Fifty-percent of anorexics in one clinic claimed they'd been sexually abused. Thirty-percent of young women raped considered suicide afterwards. Forty-one percent thought it would happen again. And eighty-two percent said it had permanently changed them. The men said they were simply being one-hundred percent men and had no reason to change.

Unsafe at Any Place

In *No Turning Back* by Estelle Freedman (Ballantine, 2002), Susan Griffin says she grew up learning that, "the world is not safe for women." Like most other women, she thought rape to be part of the natural environment—something to be feared and prayed against like fire or lightning. "I never asked why men raped; I simply thought it one of the many mysteries of human nature."

In the Army

A Department of Defense study in 2003 declared that nearly one-third of a nationwide sample of female veterans seeking health care through the V.A. had experienced rape or attempted rape during their service. Of that group, 37 percent said they were raped multiple times, and 14 percent reported they were gang-raped.

A change in DOD policy in 2005 allowing sexual assaults to be reported confidentially in "restricted reports" led to the number of reported assaults across the military rising to 40 percent. Female soldiers coming back from Iraq relate their fears of even going to the latrines in the middle of the night for the fear of being sexually assaulted. One female soldier, according to a *New York Times* story about widespread sexual harassment and rape of female U.S. soldiers by their male colleagues in Iraq, said:

> You're one of three things in the military—a bitch, a whore or a dyke. As a female, you get classified pretty quickly (Sarah Corbett, "Sunday Magazine," 3.18.07).

States Against Rape

By the 1980's twenty-three U.S. states had enacted laws against marital rape. By 1996 all states had made it illegal, but some states left room for "exceptional circumstances."

For Example

Judges still tend to blame the victim. In the 1990's a Florida judge sympathized with a male defendant, ruling that the way she dressed provoked the rape.

Incest: Protecting Men

Early in the 20th century, incest was redefined to protect the male. Girl incest victims, some as young as eight or nine-years-old, were labeled "juvenile sex delinquents" and blamed for their sexual activity.

Mothers were blamed for not protecting their daughters. The culprit was identified as the man-in-the-street, a sexual deviant or pervert, strangers to their victims. This redefinition shifted scrutiny away from the family, where the action was taking place.

Incest patterns have changed less than any other form of family violence over the last century. The myth that men are only attracted to pubescent girls is false. Almost all the victims are girls, generally under the age of ten. Twenty-five percent of American victims are under the age of five. The incest typically goes on for years, and only stops when the girl moves away, they're discovered, or because of pregnancy (or the fear of it).

Double Bind

Men defend incest as part of their paternal rights. They have sexual "needs" and their prerogative is to "have" women. Father-daughter incest creates confusion and a double bind for the girl as she tries to meet both standards of virtue: to be obedient and to be sexually pure. A balance between modesty and submission, chastity and obedience. A recipe for bi-polarity.

Men Not Protecting

According to the American Psychological Association, fathers commit one-fourth of the sexual abuse of girls, stepfathers another fourth, and most of the other perpetrators are adoptive fathers or other male relatives (*No Turning Back*).

Case in Point

In 1930, Susan, introduced to sex by her brothers when she was eight-years-old, continued to have sex with a boarder as well as with her brothers and father. When it was discovered, she was taken from the home and placed in foster homes through the State Board of Charities.

Her father got a slap on the wrist; her brothers not even that (*Heroes of Their Own Lives*, Gordon, Viking, 1988).

In another case, the chief of Police refused to question the father about assaulting his daughter because "it would be asking him to incriminate himself."

Incest Taboo: Two Types

The mid-century denial of incest was based on the incest taboo, one of the fundamental bases of civilization. But there were two versions. The taboo that everybody believed in and respected was about incestuous *breeding*. Incestuous sex *without reproductive consequences* was condemned as well, but tacitly permitted (*Heroes of Their Own Lives*). And while it may not be as common as it once was, the permissive climate surrounding it is still very much present. This allows it to continue, just as rape continues unabated, though it also is condemned.

Incest Illuminated

When the women's rights movement challenged the assumptions that conventional family life was inherently superior to alternative forms of family life, only then did incest receive the light of day. The nuclear family wasn't so safe after all.

CHAPTER 20

POLITICS OF ABORTION

At the turn of the century, even though abortion was against the law, it was not difficult for a woman to obtain an abortion in the city. In 1915, midwives delivered about half of Chicago's babies (*When Abortion was a Crime*, Reagan, 1997). Doctors performed abortion in equal numbers as midwives. However a New York study of 10,000 working-class women found that physicians had induced four times as many abortions as midwives (*Birth Control in Practice*, 1933)

Linking Midwives and Abortion

There was now a push by "Regular Doctors" (male) to eradicate abortion and to eliminate midwives from the practice of childbirth altogether. Between 1890 and 1920, the anti-midwife and anti-abortion campaign fused into one. Obstetricians, trying to establish themselves and their specialty, focused on midwives as the source of their field's low status. Midwives were usually poor immigrants, functioning within their own neighborhood. The obstetricians led a campaign to outlaw midwives.

And Prostitution

Reformers linked abortion, midwives, and prostitution. Girls who had abortions would become prostitutes (later Communists). Even though as many women died at the hands of physicians as with midwives, newspapers focused their attention on midwife-related deaths. Even when a physician was arrested for an abortion-death, midwives were still blamed, involved or not.

Early Pregnancy as a Menstrual Problem

At the turn-of-the-century, women, when pregnant, perceived their bodies as "out of order." They needed to be "fixed up," to be "put straight." Something had invaded the body and it had to be gotten rid of.

This shows the persistence of the idea that early pregnancy was a menstrual problem. It was popularly believed into the 1920's that having an abortion was a woman's right. This alternate morality existed in conflict with the law.

The High Road

By identifying midwives with abortion, physicians had an effective weapon in their crusade to bring midwives under medical scrutiny and under state control. Plus they could claim the high road in being against abortion. It made physicians appear morally upright and it shifted attention away from their own abortion practices. (*When Abortion was a Crime*).

Fear and Anxiety over Women's Sexuality

Anti-abortionists highlighted women's new sexual liberty. Women's deaths, caused by abortion attempts, emphasized the dangers of sex. The obstetrics camp prevailed: the antiabortionists channeled the anxiety over female sexuality into support for the medical profession's anxiety over midwife control. In 1908, in Chicago, midwives faced increased surveillance and new municipal codes.

Myth of Single Victim

The anti-abortionists played on the image of the poor victim, a single girl living in the city for the first time and being taken advantage of. Newspapers, prosecutors and physicians played up the abortion-related deaths of unwed women, even though *abortion was practiced by mostly married women until after WWII.*

AMA Fights Birth Control and Maternal Health

Physicians fought the new birth control movement from the mid-1910's into the 30's. They only let up when they turned their attention to the Sheppard-Towner Act in 1921. This act, a victory for the women's movement, provided matching funds to states to improve maternal and infant care. At the time, childbirth death rates in the U.S. were among the highest in the world. The AMA, fearing the loss of private-paying patients, fought the Sheppard-Towner Act as well as national health insurance (*When Abortion was a Crime).*

Illinois, home of the AMA, was one of three states that refused to participate in the Sheppard-Towner Act. Congress abolished the Act in 1929 under pressure from the AMA and from politically conservative groups. They believed healthy babies to be a Communist plot.

Abortion Insurance

During the depression years women had abortions on a massive scale. Kate Simon told of her mother's thirteen abortions, which, according to her mother, was "by no means the neighborhood record." In New Jersey, police uncovered a "Birth Control Club." Membership entitled members access to contraceptives materials and to abortion if needed.

Men Still in the Primeval Dark

Many women had the additional fear of being beaten by their husbands if they found out another kid was on the way. Countless men were still looking for the flashlight, wondering how things worked. They thought the tooth fairy brought babies.

Self-Induced Abortions

Black and white women used different techniques to induce abortion. In a study cited in *When Abortion was a Crime*, about one-half of white women's abortions were induced by a physician or midwife. African American women, not having access to doctors and midwives, were more likely to self-induce their abortions. Sometimes they had success by the ingestion of bluing and starch, or by swallowing gunpowder (rubbing it on evidently didn't work) and whiskey. Husbands tried to keep them calm and away from matches.

Economics of Birth Control

The depression helped legitimize the use of birth control. Even the AMA abandoned its official opposition to it. The depression years made vivid the relationship between economics and reproduction. Unfortunately, the Pope believed economics to be the voodoo of the devil.

Childbirth Dangerous

Women were afraid of death during childbirth. In the 1920's, 20,000 women a year died during childbirth. Obstetricians had by this time established their specialty and were afraid to ask midwives how to do it correctly.

Midwives Safer

Midwives, who had a lower rate of maternity mortality from the 1910's into the 30's, had disappeared from northern cities like

Chicago. Midwives fared better with abortion-related deaths as well. In Minneapolis, a study from 1927-1936 showed that physicians were responsible for twice as many deaths as midwives. But, the physicians said in their defense, they charged twice as much as midwives.

In 1968, in Madera, California, two midwives were hired to attend births at the county hospital after the doctors quit over pay issues. After two years, the rate of babies dying in the hospital was cut in half. Afraid of looking bad, the doctors agreed to resume attending births if the county fired the two midwives. They were fired, the doctors came back on board, and the rate of babies dying rose to the earlier level (*Born in the USA: How a Broken Maternity System Must Be Fixed to Put Women and Children First*, Wagner, University. of California, 2006).

Abortion in the 1940's and 50's

Abortion took a new turn in the 40's. The *Ladies Home Journal* urged women to "correct the mistakes" of the 20's and 30's by having numerous babies. Women had a "social obligation" to bear children. Those who didn't produce deserved to be punished. Freud equated maternity with female sexual gratification. This was another escape hatch for men, always in need of loopholes.

Repressive Atmosphere

The repression of abortion during the 1940's took new forms. Prosecutors worked to shut down the skilled abortionists, including many physicians who had operated clinics for years with little interference.

Uppity Women Need Little Ones

This intensified crack-down on abortion signaled a reaction against the apparent advances women were making and their growing independence. The assault on feminine independence began in the 1940's, after WW II when women had experienced life without men

Women faced intense social and ideological pressure to bear children. It was in the air; they were expected to be expectant.

Invasion of Body-Snatchers

The state went after the weakest people, the female victims, leaving the powerful, reputable physicians, whose names were withheld in court cases. Newspapers linked abortion to organized crime and the criminal underworld. State officials captured women and invaded their bodies, justifying it as part of their investigations into illegal abortions. Women had no rights against these involuntary invasions of their bodies.

Women Publicly Humiliated

Women were not prosecuted for having an abortion, but were punished through persistent questioning by doctors and police. The public exposure of their abortions amounted to a forced verbal pornography. Reputations were ruined and they were traumatized at having to answer publicly, information they'd be embarrassed to whisper to a close confidante. They were questioned about who, what, when, where and why: facts pertaining to the sexual encounters that led to their pregnancy. All this to publicly shame and humiliate them. And titillate the supposedly serious male pursuers of justice.

Abortion Linked to Communism

Abortion symbolized subversiveness; this tied it to Communism. The machinery of McCarthyism helped in the surveillance of abortion activities. It was part of the political and cultural attack on critical thought and behavior. For example, the Los Angeles Police Department had a six-member team devoted exclusively to pursuing abortion cases. The other six police officers were investigating slots in Las Vegas.

Therapeutic Abortions

At the time the anti-abortion laws were passed, there were provisions made for "therapeutic abortions" to be performed by physicians when deemed necessary for health reasons. When authorities thought some doctors were too lenient in their criteria, therapeutic abortions were restricted to hospitals, where a board had to review and approve each application.

During this repressive climate, the therapeutic exceptions, low to begin with, dropped sixty-five percent from 1943 to 1962. Blacks, suffering from both economic and social discrimination, found it very difficult to obtain one. In that same time span, whites in New York City had over ninety-one percent of the therapeutic abortions.

Package Deal, Sterilization Included Free-of-Charge

Approval for an abortion was often contingent on accepting sterilization, a "package" deal. At a Lying-In hospital in Chicago, sixty-seven percent of women who had a therapeutic abortion were sterilized at the same time in an eight-year period (*When Abortion a Crime*). Gynecologists around the country agreed to perform abortion only if accompanied by sterilization.

Once it Starts

The propensity to sterilize low-income women of color matched calls by public officials for the forced sterilization of poor, unmarried mothers. Puerto Rican women in NYC were surgically sterilized six times more frequently than white women.

It Expands

In 1932 there were 12,000 eugenic sterilizations. It started with the zeal to rid society of the "undesirable" and "unproductive elements." The concept of "fitness" became linked with the desire to promote social control and eliminate poverty. Hitler was watching in the wings.

Into Sex

By 1938, the sterilization policies at the Virginia Colony for Epileptics and Feeble-Minded expanded. "Sexual license" had characterized the behavior of all the women recommended for sterilization. Carrie Buck had been institutionalized there, not because she was feeble, but because she was the mother of an illegitimate child. The Bucks were also poor. In California, three of four women sterilized under the eugenics sterilization laws had been sexual delinquents (*Dubious Conceptions*, Luker, 1997).

The 1960's and the Road to Roe

In the early 60's police called abortion the third largest criminal activity in the country, after narcotics and gambling. In 1939, Cook County Hospital treated over 1,000 women for abortion-related complications. By 1959 that number had tripled, and in 1962 it was up to 5,000. Between 1951 and 1962, the number of abortion deaths had doubled.

In the early 60's, forty-two percent of maternal mortality resulted from abortion in New York City.

Change in the Air

By the late 60's the tide began to turn. The medical profession which had organized to criminalize abortion in the mid-19th century now began to oppose those very laws. The abortion laws undermined their medical autonomy.

Speak-Outs

In 1967 and '68, women's liberation groups were formed. In "consciousness-raising" groups, women learned about their sexual repression at the hands of the male-dominated society and they demanded change. At "speak-outs" they publicly proclaimed their beliefs in the right to own their bodies. They admitted publicly that they had had abortions, thus erasing the sting, shame and secrecy surrounding it. They saw it as a problem for all women arising out of the double standard.

Leading to Roe

The early skirmish on the road to Roe took place in Illinois where opponents claimed that the abortion statutes deprived women equal access to treatment available to "women of means," which violated the protection provisions of the constitution.

Then in *Griswold v. Connecticut* (1965), the U.S. Supreme Court declared a "zone of privacy existed in the marital relationship." And in 1973, in *Roe v. Wade*, the state for the first time recognized women's role and right in reproductive policy.

Sterilization Still

Women's rights group now focused on sterilization. In Alabama, Minnie Lee and Mary Alice Relf, two young black sisters aged twelve and fourteen, had been forcibly sterilized at a government-funded family planning clinic, according to D'Emillio and Freedman in *Intimate Matters*. And in Aiken, South Carolina, a mother of more than two kids had to first agree to sterilization before they would deliver her baby. She was a welfare recipient.

In 1973, fourteen states were debating legislation designed to coerce women on welfare to undergo sterilization. Government officials estimated that it funded between 100,000 and 200,000 operations per year.

Backlash on Abortion

It began in the 1980's and 90's with the denial of public funding for abortion for low-income women and federal employees. They used the fetus to shift the debate away from women and their stories about the crimes of illegal abortion. The conservative right was upset by women's sexual freedom, and the new civil rights being promulgated. The women they attacked most often were teens and low-income women.

Single women, formerly seen as victims, were now seen as sexual actors. The attacks on "welfare" and abortion were related, for both sought to control women and their reproduction. The task of parental notification, required of teens, was to punish them for their behavior. Sexism, racism, and elitism—the Holy Trinity of Patriarchy --were embedded in the twin assault on welfare and abortion.

Currently, the policy of putting the fetus ahead of the mother is making the present increasingly similar to the pre-Roe period. One-third of American women cannot locate an abortion provider in their own county. In over eighty percent of American counties, no one is provided a legal abortion (*When Abortion was a Crime*).

Can't Trust a Woman

The reversal sent a clear message: women can't be trusted to make moral decisions about children and family. They must be overseen and regulated by men. Procreation is a state mandate not a choice. Women's bodies, their lives, and their sexuality are not their own. They belong to the Company Store, the store opened in 1st century Rome by Augustus.

CHAPTER 21

FROM CHORUS GIRLS TO BARBIE: BUYING AND SELLING AMERICAN BEAUTY

Beauty, for women, becomes more important than their accomplishments. And, now that they are in the grip of beauty's artifice, they can no longer claim the "high road." Furthermore, the more women are recognized exclusively for their beauty, the cheaper they become. With competition comes a buyer's market. Women are not seen for who or what they are; they're recognized at the physical level of skin. And curves. That's their "depth" to a man's eyes. And that's how they're appraised.

The 1910's

Models had been just a step above prostitutes until a certain Mr. Powers transformed the profession, setting up the first modeling agency and attracting New York debutantes. The rise in models' esteem coincided with the rise in popularity of the chorus girl, and both helped to legitimize the beauty contest. Early contestants were judged in a number of different kinds of clothing outfits, similar to a fashion show.

Chorus Girls as Cinderella

The girls of the Floradora Sextet, a popular group at the beginning of the century, weren't discovered by Prince Charming for their foot size. The millionaires who came courting them had curves on their minds. The girls got married, one by one, and the rotating cast of the Sextet signed up new members. In 1905 there were 60,000 applicants for each opening. Since many of them came from poor homes, they gave a boost to the Cinderella myth: any woman can reach the top, as long as she looks good. The Sextet's members were famous for not having any talent.

The Cinderella myth climaxed with the beauty contest, though it took years before the Miss America contest gained acceptance. A woman exhibiting so much flesh was thought to be deranged, or at least weird. Parading half-naked before a man was unthinkable, unless you were a chorus girl. W.D. Griffith, the famous movie director, couldn't find any actress willing to show a bare ankle while walking on the beach. He had to promise the willing woman a trip to the moon before he had any volunteers. Round-trip no less.

Tough to be Short

Many beach towns passed ordinances restricting how much of a woman's arms and legs could show. When a young woman at Atlantic City wore a shortened bathing suit in 1913, she was assaulted by an angry crowd. Mad that the suit was too short to shred.

Women Find their Niche

In 1921, at Atlantic City, the Miss America Bathing Beauty was crowned. Women willingly displayed their semi-nude bodies to compete, to be looked at by men and judged by them. The beauty contest had legitimized physical beauty as the overriding feature of the ideal American woman, the semi-nude body its central symbol.

Women, according to men who were promoting the pageant, had now found their place. Men compete in sports, business, and the professions, with recognition and material rewards their goal. Women compete with their bodies and faces, marriage being their goal. By 1900, Sears advertised rouge in catalogs. It was now acceptable to use rouge sticks and powder puffs at lunch, but not at dinner (*American Beauty*). Some women simply renamed dinner lunch. Catholic women wore rouge crosses and used rosary-flavored perfume to compete.

The emphasis was on beauty and youth, a perfectly matched pair. Old age, at that time forty for a woman, meant you were ugly, crotchety, finicky, a buffoon at best. A forty-year-old man would glibly say, "I'd gladly trade my forty-year-old in for a couple of twenties." Hollywood films did their part, becoming a vast Miss America contest. A woman's film career might be over when she was thirty-years-old. Ten if she were precocious.

The 1920's and the Flapper

Women in the 20's created a new look. Called the "Flapper," she was epitomized as a stick figure with flying arms and legs. She wore short skirts, was flat-chested, and had a small face and lips (similar to the "bee-stung" look). She bobbed her hair, causing beauty parlors to mushroom from 5,000 in 1920 to 25,000 in 1925.

New "Appreciation" for Women

Girls in the 1920's were freer than ever before. They were "on the loose," on the prowl for the opposite sex. Men, on the defensive, reacted by setting up standards with which to "appreciate" women's appearances. According to Marjorie Rosen in *Popcorn Venus*, men's former gentle and appreciative criticism now became brutal, as they sought to take women down a notch. The male "club" hit them where they had made themselves vulnerable—their bodies. Men felt threatened by confident women.

Beauty for Sale

Beauty could now be bought. And sold. Cosmetics' advertisements sold the idea that an attractive appearance was something affordable and easily achieved. The 20's marked a turning point in women's use of cosmetics. As late as 1916, only one in five American women used toilet preparations; the per capita expenditure was fifty cents.

Beauty for Life

Helena Rubenstein and other entrepreneurs established a tradition of beauty culture to last a woman's lifetime. Women would find beauty by simply adopting daily rituals of skin and hair care, and by using the required products and techniques "coordinated and tailored especially for her" for the rest of her life.

Women's Duty, Again

If a woman wanted to keep her husband, it wasn't enough to keep a nice house and not bother him, now she had to stay beautiful. Annete Kellerman, the sleek swimming star proclaimed in a 1920's ad: "The first duty of women is to attract."

By promoting the idea of improving nature, women entrepreneurs validated beauty culture for a broad range of women. With the democratization of manufactured beauty, all women could improve their looks, and if they didn't, they had only themselves to blame. Guilt paved a trough to the cash register.

Have a Secret?

Lambert Pharmaceutical Company, makers of Lysol Disinfectant, made Listerine antiseptic a common household product by inventing a new disease: halitosis. Preying upon the fears and desires of its female readers, the slogan: "She looks old enough to be his mother," was enough to make every woman stock up on cases of Listerine so no one could accuse her of harboring a secret, bad breath. Some women put it on their cereal, secretly.

Turning Point: Women's Beauty No Longer Her Own

The 1920's marshaled a moment when mass-produced images distinctly and powerfully began to influence female self-confidence and beauty rituals. Women now proclaimed their liberation from the past by using cosmetics. As Lois Banner says in *American Beauty*, this period began with woman's freedom and individuality, but ended by binding her identity to something made outside her, in a factory.

Standardized Bodies

Standard sizing began in the 1920's. This of course was advantageous for the manufacturing industry. Before this, each person's clothes could be individually tailored. Sizing increased the emphasis on personal body size, and legitimated the "normative" size range. Previously, clothes had to fit the body, now that was reversed: the body had to fit the clothes. If the body didn't, it was "irregular." Standard cup sizes for women led to an increase in self-consciousness about their breasts. Now only mannequins could feel normal.

Aren't We All Alike

The infinite variety of female lives and looks was distilled into one pure image: the woman who reveals nothing but her beauty. Women studied their favorite heroines in the movies and tried to reshape their looks and their hair the same way. They bought the first home hair-permanent kits in 1934. The concept of individualized attraction had vanished in favor of conformity to a popular image. Safety in numbers. And men were in charge of the numbers.

New Merchandise

Manufacturers and consumers in the 20's and 30's increasingly perceived the female "face" as a style, subject to trends and fads.

According to *Hope in a Jar* by Kathy Peiss 1988), this offered companies a powerful rationale for introducing new products. In 1929 the *Ladies Home Journal* proclaimed the "return to feminine charm," as a fluid and elegant silhouette replaced the boyish flapper look. The *Journal* promoted this upcoming "Charm Decade" as a rich merchandising and advertising opportunity. Manufacturers gleefully shifted into overdrive, as they raced advertisers to the bank.

The 1930's: Untie the Breasts

In the 20's women's breasts and hips were reduced, while the waist was expanded from eighteen inches to twenty-four inches. The breasts were unbound in the 30's, the hemline came down, and women had a waist again. Greto Garbo and Joan Crawford portrayed the assertive, self-confident masculinized female, confident in life and love, not one to be pushed around. But no matter how strong, she had to capitulate to the man in the final frames of the movies, making it clear that men were still in charge and marriage was women's goal. Always the happy tragic ending.

Tanned Coca

Another change happened with facial color. It was now okay for the standard pale, sickly white face to be darker. Coca Chanel showed up tanned in the tabloids. Of course when autumn came, it was time to bleach the skin "back to white." The true American face was white. The melting pot of beauty types excluded African-Americans.

Some bleach was dangerous. Nadinola Skin Cream contained ten-percent ammoniated mercury that could cause serious skin irritation and damage. Many women, black and white, ruined their skin and health with bleaching.

Everyready Women

Cosmetics' ads ceaselessly reminded women that they were on display and had to be "ready" at all times. Women were urged to transform the "spectacle" of themselves into self-conscious performances. Makeup would help in this personal transformation. A woman could remake her "self," improve her life-chances simply by changing her look. In 1936, the "Makeover" was begun; the "Made-Over Girl" had arrived. She's still here.

Cosmetics as Cure-all

Good for the body, and good for the mind as well. Therapeutic language entered cosmetics' promotions in the 30's. "Beauty-In-a-Jar" will improve her "mental health and development." If she doesn't update her looks, she might "destroy some of her potential personalities lurking beneath the surface." Lipstick cured neurosis. Psychiatrists set up shop in beauty salons.

Good for Marriage

Cosmetics were seen as talismans, as weapons to be employed in pursuit of men and marriage. Some women made necklaces out of Noxzema jar-tops as a trap.

Putting On at College

"Paint," once denounced as "prostitute's grease," was now celebrated as "glamorous," one of the thrill words of the decade. For young college or working women, "putting on a face" had become a daily ritual, part of dressing. Without her "face," she felt naked. It was part of her personality. At Smith College, guidance counselors noted women's "attractiveness" in their records.

At the Company

Employment tests appraised a woman's "bodily appearance." The Heinz Company had weekly manicures for the female pickle packers. They were so popular that they expanded the program, instructing workers on proper makeup. The pickles got packed prettier.

Rules for When and Where

Once makeup was widely accepted, advertisers and beauty experts regulated its use by trafficking in subtle distinctions. Rouge: okay on the dance floor, not in the office; lipstick: not okay before mid-afternoon. Face whiteners: okay for hunting rabbits, not moose.

Now that women knew how to use makeup, based on time of day, activity, age, height, square root of weight divided by hair curls, beauty reporters used these as criteria, crucial to the cycle of fashion. Magazines continue this practice today, scheduling star and starlet breakups to coincide with the changing seasons, starlets' babies landing on Christmas, especially if it's a virgin birth.

Globalization of American Beauty: the 1940's

By 1940, manufactured beauty formed a major sector of the economy and it was part of women's everyday practices. The made-up woman of the 40's was a global commodity, a symbol exported in movies and promoted by cosmetics firms. She was an illustration of the American way of life. And, away from home, pin-ups reminded the soldiers of women's service to the national ideals.

Patriotic Lipstick

Even before Pearl Harbor, journalists worried that a "glamour shortage" would seriously lower the national morale. During WW II, cosmetics' ads pointed out that lipstick "symbolized one of the reasons why we are fighting, the precious right of women to be feminine and lovely." Women wore lipstick as a badge of courage which signified the "red blood of the true American woman" (*Hope in a Jar*). Blue would come later.

Lipstick enabled women to "do" as a man, "appear" as a woman. Tangee Lipstick equated the protection of freedom and democracy with the protection of beauty. Indelible lips all-of-a-sudden became important, a new fashion twist. Bishop introduced lipstick that "stays on you, not him." It made makeup less of an artifice. Later on, they charged extra to put the "lip smear" back in.

On the Playing Field

The All-American Girls Professional Baseball League, organized during the war, ordered the players to take makeup lessons from Helena Rubenstein and to appear "ladylike" on the field (*Hope in a Jar*). They had to stop at the "rouge station" located on each base. Home runs could take up to an hour.

Charm Classes at Boeing Aviation

In the factories, cosmetics again played an important role. Psychological and efficiency experts testified to the importance of cosmetics in combating fatigue, improving morale and increasing productivity. Lockheed installed beauty salons and cosmetics stations. Boeing offered charm classes in its factories (*Hope in a Jar*). Women workers received special commendation for the attention they paid to grooming. But no raises.

Women still had to be careful they didn't tread on men's prerogatives. Nell Giles, who worked in an armaments factory, described being hooted down by male workers for carrying a black tin lunch box. Nell received a gallon of pink paint the very next day.

Victory!

It worked. American women won the beauty war. By 1948, eighty to ninety per-cent of adult American women used lipstick, sixty-five percent used rouge, and twenty-five percent wore eye makeup. Men emerged from the trenches.

Sex-in-Advertising,

In the early 1950's the sexual motif became more explicit in advertising. Women were urged to make themselves beautiful to catch "his attention," to awaken "his desire." Fire and Ice (Revlon, 1952) cleverly used a little quiz to ask a woman what "type" was she, one who played with fire? Or one who liked making ice cubes?

Clairol came up with the, "Does she or doesn't she," ostensibly about hair dye. Maidenform bra stopped women in their tracks with, "I dreamed I stopped traffic" ads.

Sexual allure and sexual desire were celebrated as key attributes of the female psyche.

Teens Too

Teens were eager converts. Noxzema developed "Cover Girl" makeup for teens. "Cover Girl" was for "nice girls," not those tarts who used Revlon. Social scientists reported that the quality teenage girls most wanted to change was their physical appearance. Followed by their psychic appearance.

Teen-Boppers Break Piggy Banks

Teenage girls anticipated their passage to womanhood by using makeup. By the mid-60's, though only eleven percent of the population, they were buying twenty-five percent of all cosmetics and beauty preparations. Some schools forbade the use of makeup in the restroom. If they smuggled makeup in their lunchboxes, they had to eat it.

Ads Sell

Ad revenue zoomed up. In the 1950's, eighty percent of cosmetics' budget went into advertising (*Beauty Myth*), twenty percent went into packaging. The rest went into the actual product.

Dumb Blondes are Smarter

Two models vied for the attention of men in the 50's: the childlike sweetheart, represented by Debbie Reynolds or Sandra Dee, and the voluptuous heart-beater Marilyn Monroe. Three out of ten women dyed their hair blonde, imitating Marilyn. The "dumb blonde" won: women accepted a model that made them feminine, sensual, and unintellectual, willing to act like children, yet express their adulthood sexually.

Career Women as Aliens

Meanwhile, back in the kitchen, housewives' virtues were sung. Career women, pictured as dangerous or neurotic, were crucified. Women's magazines glamorized the home. Wasn't the war fought so that women could return to the home? The articles urged women to make contact with "your ideal self": that part of you that aspires to be a good wife, mother and efficient homemaker. This was the age of contact with aliens.

Fashions for the 50's featured skirts to the mid-calf held out by starched crinoline petticoats, or skirts so tight that walking was difficult. Waists were held in by girdles, called "minimizers," and strengthened at the waist with concrete supports and steel beams. For evening: boned, tightly-laced corsets, called "merry widows." Breasts were supported to enhance their size, padding was common. Most brassieres were wired or boned to hold breasts rigid and straight, bring them to points and accentuate the nipples. Miss-guided missiles.

Shoes came to a sharp point resulting in pinched toes. That plus the three-inch heel (standard equipment), made walking difficult. Naturally physical education and sports were out, but girls could exercise themselves through cheerleading and by being pom-pom girls.

Bring on the Babies

The push for babies that started in the 1940's bore fruition in the 50's. Women who married in the 50's had their first child earlier than their grandmothers. During the 40's and 50's women married younger, had more kids sooner, and bore more kids than at any time in the 20th century. Between 1940 and 1960, women of childbearing age raised the ideal number of kids from two to four. Before puberty.

Why Wait till High School?

By the end of the 50's, the marriage age had dropped into the teens. Fourteen million girls were engaged by the age of seventeen. Girls were getting married in high school, going steady at twelve and thirteen years-of-age. Brassieres with false bosoms of rubber for girls as young as ten were now being sold.

A New Degree

The proportion of women attending college dropped from forty-seven percent in 1920 to thirty-five percent in 1958. A century earlier, women had fought to get into college to get a degree, now they went to get a husband. By the mid-50's, sixty percent dropped out of college to marry or because they were afraid too much education would hurt them in the marriage market. There was now a new degree, the Ph.T, putting your husband through college (*The Feminine Mystique,* Betty Freidan, 1963*)*.

New Career for Women

By the end of the 1950's, the U.S. birthrate was overtaking India's. The birth-control movement, renamed Planned Parenthood, was asked to find a method whereby women who'd been advised that a 3rd or 4th baby would be born defective, might still agree to have it. College women were now having four, five and six kids instead of two, making a career out of having babies.

Back to Nature

The 1960's also brought the "natural" look. Women gave up red lips and nail polish; straight hair was in. Cosmetics firms and magazines publishers were confused, not knowing how long it would be before women got back to their senses. Men were more confused than usual; women were not buying their script.

Twiggy and Barbie

In the 60's, fashion photographers decided stick-thin bodies would put more emphasis on the clothes. Twiggy was perfect. At 5'6' and 97 lbs., she was the ideal model as well as the natural prototype for Barbie: a model in 1959, career girl in 1963, surgeon in 1973, and an aerobics instructor in 1984. Through it all, Barbie retained her misshapen body: exaggerated breasts, long legs, and non-hips.

Career Women Seen as Threat

Barbie was the antithesis of the 1950's mother, a radical role model. As a career girl in 1963, she raised alarm bells with advertisers. They feared the numerical rise of career women whose intelligence would make them too critical to be ideal customers. Better to push pregnancy than college and a career.

Women not only questioned their appearance, they wondered who or what was behind it—who was telling women to appear pleasing to men? They were getting to the heart of the matter, the boardroom.

Feminists Confront their Oppression

Feminists condemned the commercialization of beauty. As Kathy Peiss pointed out in *Hope in a Jar*, they saw the connection between beauty and the marketplace. Female desires and anxieties were manipulated in order to control women and keep them subservient to men. Feminists faced the fact that they were driven into absorption with appearance, into making themselves objects of display for men.

Sex Sells

The 60's guide book for women was *Sex and the Single Girl*, by Helen Gurly Brown (1962). The idea was to help the urban girl navigate the new terrain she'd staked out for herself. But the marketplace had its own ideas and began using her self-proclaimed sexuality to sell products. The sexualized mystique of the airline stewardess, the model, and the executive secretary were promoted simultaneously. The Man was re-gaining control of his minions.

Sex Doesn't Sell

The consumer culture is manipulated to drive a wedge between men and women, to make women feel estranged within their own bodies, and to fuel the carnage that erupts within relationships. Sexual estrangement between men and women is what sells, as sold by Naomi Wolfe in *The Beauty Myth,* Anchor, 1991*)*. Men and women have to be convinced, over and over, that they're at war. Ads sell sexual discontent.

Consumer culture depends on maintaining a broken line of communication between women and men. If they got along amicably, the stock market would crash, the pope would need a new job, and prisons would become mausoleums. Beauty pornography helps to maintain this unequal equilibrium by putting women on edge. Men are along for the ride, as well as being in the driver's seat.

Dressing for Work

Suddenly, part of the job requirement, for women, was to look good. All the professions that women were making strides in had been reclassified as "display" professions, formerly restricted to fashion mannequins, dancers, actresses and highly-paid sex workers. Now garbage-collecting, coal mining, and house maids required sexy outfits. Their tailored business suits didn't make the cut (and the men-run fashion industry zipped that closed after the first season). They found themselves forced to dress femininely, but not "too femininely," provocatively, but not "too provocatively." Sexual harassment suits replaced women's former business suits.

Dress Codes

Employers began telling female employees how to dress. This happened when women began to proliferate in the workplace and questions arose about their appearance. At a company in Britain, if women refused to wear sexually exploitive costumes to work, they could lose their job. In the U.S., "beauty" was ruled to be something that could legally gain or lose women their jobs. Men tried to get it inserted into the wedding vows.

Harassment

Two-thirds to nine-tenths of women experienced harassment at their workplace. This they blamed on themselves for not controlling their appearance. Sexual harassment and rape by employers was often excused for employers because the woman was attractive. In *Diaz v. Coleman* an employer was exonerated in a sexual harassment suit because the employees wore short skirts, part of his dress code.

Craft Changes Course

In 1983 Christine Craft was fired from Metro Media in Kansas City, for being too old, unattractive and not deferential enough to men. She was thirty-six years-old. She filed a lawsuit. Two juries found for her; however a male judge overturned the verdict. Women everywhere were put on notice. The profession of "image consultant" grew eightfold over the next decade. Women, work, and beauty outside the sex professions fused on the day Craft lost her case.

Women Measure Down

Advertising has played a role in undermining women's self-confidence. When female nudes appeared in *Vogue* for the first time in the 1970's, women had graphic details of perfection against which to measure themselves. Women began to scrutinize their bodies and to connect it to feminine sexual pleasure. They believed they had to have *that* face, *that* body to achieve *that* ecstasy. They'd have to *look* that way to *feel* that way.

Porn does Part

Pornography plays its part, soft and hard. Soft pornography objectifies the female body. Hard porn does violence to it. Women become cut off from their bodies. They no longer own them. It's not uncommon for women to be "separated" from their bodies during the act of love.

Hard-core porn helped spawn violence and sado-masochism towards women in the 1980's. Ads for Saab with the camera looking up her thigh: "Don't worry. It's ugly underneath." (Where are the Knights of the Holy Garter?) In *Vogue,* some Doberman Pinschers attack the model. In another ad a woman sits up and begs, her wrists tied with a leash. And these are the ones for preschoolers.

Supreme Court, 1986

In a narrow ruling, the U.S. Supreme Court made sexual harassment illegal. But it also permitted a woman's speech or dress to be cited as relevant "sexual provocation."

It wasn't easy for women to win harassment suits. To be credible about being harassed, a woman had to look harrassable, and that would destroy her credibility.

The 70's: Still Natural

Makeup was used sparingly by women; some gave it up altogether. But curls, permanents, and eye makeup flourished. When women were warned that hair dyes could cause cancer, the use of hair dyes dropped a measly four percent.

Eyes on the Prize

Manufacturers embraced the "natural look" with organic cosmetics. They invoked the "liberated" woman as a beauty type. "Charlie" perfume was for this new "type" of beauty. Clinique started to distribute makeup as "information." Mary Kay fused the recent feminine economic gains with traditional ideals of womanhood. Now that women have more power and money, don't they deserve a big house? With ten kids to exert power over?

CHAPTER 22

EATING AND WEIGHT: SHOPPING FOR SHAPE

During the course of the 20th century, the ideal body shape for women has shifted dramatically, becoming thinner and thinner to suit social and economic needs. As her body has been sliced and spliced to meet the latest fashion expectations, her looks have had to keep pace with the latest definition of "beauty," as defined by the latest magazine models and lingerie mannequins. Up to two-thirds of women do not like their bodies. Mannequins are noted for their lack of "unsightly body hair."

Articles on dieting bulged in the 1980's. In the previous decade, women had made the most significant gains since Cleopatra, and men were scared of their heft. By 1989, there were over three hundred diet books on the market, each one invoking another strand of guilt for women to grapple with.

And they've been convinced. Ninety per-cent of women in a 1985 survey think they weigh too much. It hurts them physically as well: one-fifth of women who exercise to shape their bodies have menstrual irregularities and diminished fertility.

The Skinny on Erotica

It's well known that plumper women desire sex more; they outscore women on the erotic scale two to one (*The Beauty Myth*). Women who diet at 1,700 calories a day cease being sexual (that's 500 calories more than the Beverly Hills Diet). At 1100 calories, they can't spell sex.

Miss America: Withering Away

A generation ago, the average model weighed eight percent less than the average American woman. Today she weighs twenty-three percent less (*The Beauty Myth*, 1991). The weight of Miss America has plummeted from eleven-percent below the national average in 1970 to seventeen-percent below in the next eight years. Nowadays they have to be tied down if there's a breeze. Since 1939, American women have gone down three to four sizes.

For women, thinness suggests feminine weakness, asexuality and hunger. This to reassure men, often in need of reassurance.

Adolescents and Eating

Seventeen, founded at the start of the school year in 1944, announced that being overweight is a medical problem. Adolescent girls began to have eating problems.

Anorexia nervosa is the characteristic psychopathology of female adolescents today. When we live in a culture that offers diet and exercise as a coherent philosophy of self, anorexia nervosa seems a sensible choice (*Fasting Girls,* Joan Brumberg, 2000*)*. Compulsory exercise and dieting are the twin obsessions. The message is: do these and you'll be thin, thus joining the ranks of the beautiful, the good, the sexy.

Anorexic girls, the majority of whom have been sexually abused, see the refusal of food as a way to remain childlike and forestall sexual development. It's a protection from sexual harassment.

Dieting Harmful

But dieting brings on its own problems. It may cause both eating disorders and obesity by provoking obsessive behavior (being one itself). Dieting and "slimming" (Great Britain) are self-inflicted semi-starvation. In India, the very poorest women eat 1,400 calories a day, 600 more than Western women on the Hilton Head Diet.

Never too Early

It's starting earlier, rampant by the 4th and 5th grades. A San Francisco survey showed that thirty-one percent of nine-year-olds thought they were too fat. And eighty-one-percent of ten-year-olds were dieters. Kindergarteners think they're balloons and walk around with strings dragging on the ground.

Hunger as Sexual Entree

Hunger is already being eroticized for today's little girls as an entry into adult sexuality. Beauty pornography makes an eating disease seem inevitable, even desirable if a young woman is to consider herself sexual and valuable. Eighty percent of prepubescent girls, as young as eight and nine-years-old, restrict eating to stay thin.

Higher Eating Problems

On college campuses, half the women suffer at some time from bulimia or anorexia nervosa. More than 150,000 American women die each year from anorexia nervosa. Five to fifteen-percent of hospitalized cases die; and fifty percent never recover completely. Ninety to ninety-five percent of Anorexics and bulimics are women.

At a typical college, of ten women, two are anorexic, six are bulimic. The norm for a young, middle-class American woman is to suffer from an eating disease.

Women's magazines say that sixty percent of American women have serious trouble eating. A survey in May, 2005 found the number of eating disorders among women over thirty-five was up thirty-three percent in three years time.

Two-Thirds to Operate On

The prime of life, from forty to sixty, is cast as men's peak years and as women's decline. One-third of a woman's life is marked with aging. And one-third of her body is made of fat—both of these conditions are transformed into operable conditions.

Surgeons depend for their profit on warping female self-perceptions and on multiplying female self-hatred. Good and evil become thin and fat, fighting for women's soul. The surgeons are the high priests, deciding women's fate. Just as doctors turned a profit with hysteria at the turn-of-the-century, now they use hysteria to do the same.

Don't Let It Show: Pregnancy and Food

Today women worry about eating and weight the way our forefathers and their doctors worried about women's sexuality. There was the terror that it "will show," and the desperate efforts to purge the "evidence."

Sexual impurity laws gave way to oral impurity taboos. Women were genitally chaste for God; now they're orally chaste for the God of Beauty.

Anti-Wrinkle Creams Worry Women

Men die once, women die twice: the death of their body is preceded by the death of their beauty. Beauty is not bestowed randomly. There are over 1,700 different anti-wrinkle creams, each "vowing to release the luminescence trapped under those icky old dead skin cells." Women are spending twelve billion dollars a year on "emollients designed to make them conformists with the perfect complexions" (*Are Men Necessary*? Maureen Dowd, 2005). To live in a world of magic, prayer and superstition makes sense.

Do They Work?

No one really believes that beauty products work. Anita Roddick of Body Shop: there's "no application that will get rid of grief or stress or heavy lines…nothing that will make you look younger. Nothing." Or Professor Kligman who developed Retin-A: "In the industry today, fakery is replacing puffery."

Crows Feet and Character: Different Hieroglyphics of Lines

The passage of time carves character on a man's face; on a woman's face it carves flawed lines and crow's feet. Eventually women internalize the notions of beauty, and they're no longer sure if they can be interesting or worthy without it.

What does Age Look Like?

What to do with Age? Airbrush it away! It's now routine. Hardly any picture of a woman today goes untouched. Photos of older women are avoided. Readers of magazines have no idea what a sixty-year-old face looks like in print. It's made to look forty-five. To airbrush age off a woman's face is to erase her identity, her power, her history.

The alternative to believing the fraud is too scary. As Naomi Wolfe says in *The Beauty Myth*, women might "accept their aging, then admire it, and finally enjoy it." There goes the economy. And men would have to at last have a look in the mirror. Their goes national security.

Beauty is Precious

Urban professional women spend up to a third of their income for "beauty maintenance." African-American women spend three to five times more on personal-care products than white Americans. The high price of cosmetics is itself a lure, part of the attraction. Beauty can't be bought easily, cheaply. It must cost an arm or a leg. Or part of a thigh.

Women Ingrained

Now it's not just the misogynists hating women; women hate themselves. Hite found that one in seven women thought the vagina was "ugly," that it smelt "bad." This leads women to shy away from physical intimacy. Bring back those Knights of the Garter (not the ones from Columbus).

In a market-driven economy, someone has to be responsible for getting the goods off the shelves. Women, ever the helpful servants in running the show, do double duty: keeping-the-stores-open by keeping-their-bodies-humming, and, at the same time, keeping their men up-and-running by keeping themselves on the sidelines. Not wanting to drain the economy or drain their men, they step up to the plate. Again and again.

Chapter 23

Surgery: The Ultimate Makeover

There are multiple ways to mortify aging flesh: cutaneous laser resurfacing, ultrasound liposuction, acid and chemical peels; $250-a-session Velasmooth treatments, combining suction and laser, to reduce cellulite; hair-removal lasers, and the latest laser craze, Fraxeling. This is a machine that emits beams of light to vaporize lines and brown spots on the neck, chest and hands for $3000 per-session. Then there's "thread lifts," in which barbed threads are stretched beneath the cheeks and anchored to the skull. If all that fails, tiny bunker-bombs can be inserted beneath the nails. Hard to know where to start.

Everybody Wants a Piece

Of the action. There are crossover gastroenterologists doing liposuction, gynecologists doing laser surgery and dentists doing breast implants. Seven states allow dentists to do cosmetic surgery. Psychiatrists claim they can erase interior memory lines.

Victorianism to Victoria's Secrets

In the 19th century a woman expressed herself sexually through *clothes* that emphasized her body shape: a tiny waist, an exaggerated bosom, and buttocks a block long.

The 20th century focused on the woman's *body* itself. Men's standards are crowd-driven and ad-driven. People today consume more ads per day than calories, most of them involuntarily. Studies prove that ads add weight.

Victorian medicine treated pregnancy, masturbation, and menopause as diseases, menstruation as a chronic disorder, and childbirth as a surgical event. Once you reached menopause, your thoughts turned to caskets. Modern medicine treats healthy bodies as if they're diseased. Parts of them need to be cut out or re-arranged. This represents a new phase of medical coercion, a reclassification of *well and beautiful women* as *sick and ugly (The Beauty Myth).* A dictionary makeover.

Changing Criteria

Just as the criteria for removing the clitoris in the nineteenth century was at first narrowly defined for women with medical problems, then broadened to include behavioral problems, the criteria for a face-lift today have expanded to include women in their 20's as a "preventative" procedure. Surgeons are now handing out leaflets in delivery rooms for baby-fat removal.

Ovariotomies became a fashionable operation in the nineteenth century, as normal women fell prey to the knife. The surgeon showed off his trophies in that era, his ovaries-on-a-platter. The sexual surgeon today displays his reconstructed wife at a cocktail party.

Cut Her up to Heal Her

Normal female sexuality was a disease in the 19th century. The role of the gynecologist was to detect and punish "sexual diseases," also seen as social crimes. Pelvic surgery could cure the disease of orgasm by destroying it. Victorian clitordectomy made women stop masturbating or stay married. In 1989 a woman was tricked into genital mutilation, inflicted without her consent by a surgeon, convinced he could improve her orgasms by surgical reconstruction (as seen on Oprah). Didn't work. Now she wants to operate on him.

Hysteria Re-visited

Once the belief that a woman's orgasm was necessary for conception was laid to rest, a woman's sexual pleasure was superfluous. The inability of women to orgasm, referred to as "hysteria," continued to be a problem. And, given the pronouncements of the day, it's no surprise.

Frigid Women

In the first decade of the 20th century, Havelock Ellis, one of the eminent spokesmen of the day, claimed that sexual anesthesia was "natural" in women. At the time, frigidity rates were sixty-six percent to seventy-five percent for "civilized" women. And it wasn't men's fault. Medical authorities in the 19th century blamed women. If women didn't reach orgasm during intercourse, they were flawed or suffered from some other impairment. All of a sudden the majority of women were defined as abnormal or frigid (*The Beauty Myth*). And they were out in the cold for a long time.

Men are Truly Amazing

Men, who despite the raging successes of the Industrial Revolution, the Age of Science, and the Renaissance and Enlightenment, despite all of this wealth of knowledge of the physical world and outer space and their probing assessment of the inner workings of the body and mind—still seemed to enter the boudoir in the dark, with blindfolds.

In *Obstetrics and Gynecology*, a medical text used in sixty of the nation's medical schools as recently as 1975, frigidity is defined as the "occasional failure to obtain orgasm," placing ninety-nine percent of women in the category of abnormal. The normal sexual act, for women, is said to entail a "masochistic surrender to the man…there is always an element of rape."

Rhythmotherapy: All the Rage

As hysteria carried over from the 19th into the 20th century, the standard treatment was pelvic massage. But "hysterical paroxysm" took a long time, up to an hour, so doctors were ecstatic when vibrators were invented. This new procedure known as "Rhythmotherapy" took only five to ten minutes, greatly increasing doctors' profits. Beauty parlors competed with doctors for the business (*Technology of Orgasm*, Johns Hopkins, 1999). Car-hops at drive-ins were instructed in the finer points.

As Seen on T.V.

They'd have been advertised on T.V. if it was around. In 1918, the Sears, Roebuck and Company's *Electrical Goods* catalog offered six models of vibrator, plus the vibratory attachment for a home motor. Ads stated the connection with nature. The "perfect woman…oscillates in union with the natural law of being."

The use of vibrators was commonly accepted during the first three decades of the 20th century, according to Rachel Maines in *The Technology of Orgasm*. They went out of fashion once women gained a better understanding of sexuality, not to mention their depiction in stag films, which blew their "health" cover. They were no longer advertised in respectable magazines from 1930 to 1970.

Ugly and Sick: From 19th to 20th century

In the 19th century, normal female activity, like working, speaking in public or education, was classified as ugly and sick. Education, they were told, would sterilize them, make them sexually unattractive, ill, cause cancer, turn them into nymphomaniacs and lead to suicide. Otherwise it was good. In the 20th century, normal female bodies are classified as ugly or sick, in need of repair (*The Beauty Myth*).

Since women today are capable of having extra-marital affairs and of asking for divorce—both threats to men's sense of security—men have upped the ante correspondingly, now requiring women to not only distrust their bodies, but to accept painful surgical alterations.

Corsets to Botulism

From Victorian corsets to Victoria Secret's "buoyant water bras" and "peppermint-stinging lip plumpers," women have always striven to look younger, prettier, healthier. But, forty years after the dawn of feminism, the ideals of feminism are more rigid and unnatural than ever. Entitled women of a certain age are filled with cow-ass fat, bioengineered botulism spores and various heavy machinery petroleums. They don't have to live on a farm, they are a farm (*Are Men Necessary?*).

Beauty Industry

In 2004, according to Alex Kuczynski (*Beauty Junkies,* 2006), there were nearly twelve million surgical and non-surgical beauty procedures performed in the US—including 290,000 eyelid jobs, 478,000 liposuctions and 334,000 breast augmentations. Though one-third of the US's artificial breasts are "in trouble," implants are up 147% since 1997. Liposuction's up 111%, tummy tucks 144%; and Botox use, 2,446%. The anti-aging market went from $1 billion-a-year in 1990 to $15 billion in 2005.

Teens Do Their Part

Paris Hilton asked in *Elle Girl* (2005), "Should teens get plastic surgery? We investigate the new trend." Teens are the fastest growing market. The number of cosmetic surgeries performed on people eighteen and under reached 74,000 in 2003, a fourteen percent increase from 2000.

An Ugly Role

Modern cosmetic surgeons have a direct financial interest in a new social role for women—one that requires them to feel ugly. As Eve Ensler has stated, it's no accident that you feel this way. There's a "plan to make you feel ugly and powerless, insignificant and insecure" (*Insecure at Last*).

To help them in this self-evaluation, advertisers, doctors, fashion and beauty magazines direct women to problems they should have. This is creative marketing. If women suddenly stopped feeling ugly, this modern branch of lucrative medicine would soon wither and be as dead as cellulite. And, if women are not "healthy" enough to believe they're ugly, they can be shipped to re-programming centers in Eastern Europe.

Masochism Addicts

As Kuczynski reveals in *Beauty Junkies*, women hate themselves; they find their bodies disgusting. And there's no end to the marketing of new procedures to fix "their problems." Now that they've botched up so many upper lip operations, they've moved further down, doing labioplastic operations on the vagina, to "tighten it up," remove excess debris, and put in a neat, carpeted landing strip.

Health supplements devote half or more of their space for fasts, fat farms, weight-loss camps, teflon surgery, breast enlargement, breast ensmallment, nipple replacement, nipple valve-jobs, eating replacement, cellulite reduction, cellulite increase, thigh curvature, and toenail-stretching (for higher-echelon pain addicts).

If it's Dead, Kill It

Surgeons call the tissues on a woman's body "dead" so they can charge her for killing them. "Cellulite" is the new enemy. An invented condition imported by *Vogue* in 1973, cellulite is now disfiguring, unhealthy, and "polluted with toxins." Before 1973, it was normal female flesh. Now it's carcinogenic.

Save that Cellulite

Women with big hips and thighs have liposuction procedures. Some have precision liposuction, recommended in *Bazaar*, to remove extra fat stored in all sorts of creases, crevices, and mountains. Some doctors, knowing a woman will come to her senses, stores the cellulite on ice, in order to have it ready for tacking back on with super-glue when she comes back.

Queen of Fat

Dr. Wexler of Manhattan takes fat from the buttocks and hips and reinjects it into facial lines, depressions and lips. Women don't seem to be worried about the alarming increase in Death by Liposuction. As Ms. Dowd explains, the 1950's woman vacuumed; today's woman is vacuumed.

Reproduction is Counter-Productive

Today's beauty surgeons define as illness any evidence on the body of its reproductive activity: stretch marks, sagging breasts, and post-partum weight. Post-partum breasts are said to be "atrophied."

AMA Takes a Stand

The AMA has become preoccupied with beauty. The maintenance of beauty is the same as the maintenance of health. Ugliness is a health issue, not a cosmetic one. Another version of the double standard: a man's thigh is for walking; a woman's thigh is for looking beautiful, then for walking.

Today's "peeling parlors" use acid to cause 2nd degree burns on s woman's face, sometimes by operatives with no medical training. Ninety per-cent of cosmetic surgery in the U.S. is performed in unregulated doctor's offices (*The Beauty Myth*). The other ten per-cent in tattoo parlors.

Botox

The only hidden chemical weapon found in Iraq was a vial of Botox, a botulism neurotoxin classified as a WMD. It's poisonous but popular. And it erases wrinkles. Since it won FDA approval in 2002, it has helped millions of people, some as young as twenty, up to men and women in their 80's. It erases faces, freezing their features, some to the point of freakish death masks, by shooting them up with Botox.

Stepford Wives Come Back

In certain locales, it's rare to see a woman over thirty-five years-of-age with the ability to look angry. T.V. producers gave up on doing a Cher show when they realized her one-expression-fits-all wouldn't work.

Frequent–Massacre Cards

Some clinics offer these cards so Botox addicts can rack up rewards. The treatments, which run from $500 to $1,500 a session and take ten minutes, need to be repeated as they are only good for six months. Botox use is up 2,446% since 1997.

Breasts Lose Shape and Size

The Officially Accepted Breast, according to the NOCP (The National Organization of Couch Potatoes) is that of an adolescent. In 1973 twenty-five percent of American women were unhappy with the size or shape of their breasts. In 1986 the number was up to thirty-three percent. The breasts themselves hadn't changed. Now it's up to one-hundred and ten percent, and the breasts are still the same, even more so.

Mannequins Now Need Implants

Surgeons performed 1.3 million breast augmentations and lifts in the last decade, a two-hundred and fifty-seven percent increase since 1997 (American Society of Aesthetic Plastic Surgery). The high-fashion industry is struggling to catch up to the new plastic silhouette. Store mannequins are getting plastic breast implants to match the overblown curves of the customers. It's skewing the selection of designer clothes and making it more difficult to buy a bra without padding.

Further Control

Allure news bulletin: "Biomecanica's battery-powered suction bra builds a bigger breast."

Adjustable Control

Over a million American women have had their breasts cut open and sacs of chemical gel implanted. This leads to a hardening of the scar tissue around these implants in seven out of ten cases. They must then be reopened and removed or the lumps have to be torn apart by the bare hands and weight of the doctor pressing down. Now a woman can have adjustable implants. For her adjustable boyfriends.

Mutilation

Breast surgery is a form of sexual mutilation. It will probably have an adverse affect on a woman's erotic stimulation (*The Beauty Myth*). With breast repositioning, the nipples become numb, without feeling. And sometimes they're hard to find—even the doctor forgets where he put them.

Disabled are Happier with Their Bodies

In this Surgical Age, the American Dream has come true. Seen as feminist liberation, a woman can now purchase her beauty with cash and the pay-as-you-pain plan. We've gone from "anything-can-be-done" to "everything-must-be-done." Fully able women of today are less satisfied with their bodies than are disabled people (*Beauty Myth).*

Just a Nip and a Tuck

Surgical brochures downplay the pain, the risks and suffering. They couch it in infantile terms: a "tummy-tuck." a "nip." And they emphasize the career pressure to look "youthful." In some upscale communities an older woman may feel out of place if she hasn't had the skin of her throat cut. Many models regard a session with the plastic surgeon as part of the job requirement. The "ideal" has become fully inhuman. A woman can no longer envisage her body free of pain and still desirable.

Plastic Emotions

When the *Valley of the Dolls* was written, Hollywood actresses went to seedy motels to find their fix. Now doctors and the pharmaceutical industry sweet-talk patients into feel-good pills on T.V and in the office. This is the Ambien generation, when being turned on takes a back seat to being turned off, as Ms. Dowd puts it. Take your pick: Prozac, Zoloft, Xanex, Wellbutrin, Paxil, Klonopin, Vicodin, Ativan, Valium, Effexor, Lexapro, they're all available—never mind the side effects—with more on the way. Need an antidepressant cause you shop too much? Try Celexa.

More Abused than Hard Stuff

In a Columbia University report (July 2005), we learn that the abuse of painkillers, stimulants and tranquilizers is more prevalent than the abuse of heroin or cocaine. Fifteen million Americans abuse prescription drugs. Two million of those are adolescents.

Women More Vulnerable

There are twice as many women depressed as men, true in most cultures. Women take more pills. They are hormonally more complicated and biologically more vulnerable than men. Women attach more willingly in relationships, and they are punished more severely when they lose an attachment. Men notice a few weeks later, if it's pointed out.

Pre-Surgical to Post-Surgical

Healing and tending the sick were female skills until the 18th-century. The profession of medicine in the 19th century barred women from their traditional healing role. Doctors were now in charge. They defined women much as Aristotle, Augustine and Thomas Aquinas had done centuries earlier: unfinished males.

In those days, women *were* their ovaries. Their minds were of little consequence, if they had any. Their ovaries caused them to be unstable and to suffer from hysteria. They were defined as sick and as potentially sickening to men.

Today women are identified with their beauty. We've gone from ovarian determinism to beauty determinism. The doctors are in charge, to impose upon woman what society needs from them. Women today need to be so preoccupied with beauty that they have no time or energy left to cause a problem for men. Like claiming to be human beings or other extravagant notions.

Professional Woman at Loss

With men who are "moving up, now marrying down," there's an epidemic of professional women missing out on husbands and kids. An Ann Hewlett survey in 2002 found that fifty-five percent of thirty-five-year-old career women were childless. It had doubled for those in the forty to forty-four-year-old bracket in twenty years.

A report from four British Universities found that the prospect for marriage increased by thirty-five percent for guys with each sixteen-point increase in their IQ. There was a forty-percent drop for each sixteen-point increase for women. Highly educated women tend to put off marriage, kids, and they're also on the waiting list to Mars, today's convent equivalent.

Women's Lib: So Over

Five years ago, high-powered women fantasized about having a *Wife* to do the shopping, cook and carpool so that she could focus on work. Now, according to Dowd in *Are Men Necessary*, she wants to *be* that Wife. They look back with longing at their mother's retro lifestyle. They want to be Mrs. Somebody, to have a baby and stay home. Women are beat. If men could be said to have a strategy, we would have to conclude that it's working: women don't want to be feminists, nor are they interested in being "liberated." What's the point? Done there, been that.

SUMMARY

The patriarchal model that began in the Old Testament, that was rubber-stamped by the Reformation, passed on by the Enlightenment and the founders of the U.S.A., is still with us today. Women are still valued as ornamental, a trophy for the rich, a catch to decorate a teenager's hotrod with, and a hotty to pamper a spotty ego. It's still about ownership and the need to prop up a weak, bleak, ego.

Today's economy depends on women remaining in their subservient state. All the succession of fashions, cosmetics, hair styles and crèmes and lotions, and now surgery over her entire body—all this fuels the economy. If women were granted a clean bill of health, it would be Armageddon on Wall Street, America's street address. Men and women relations—as unhealthy and in need of fixing-up as women's bodies are said to be--are clamped in an economic vise-grip. To extricate them from their market-bound, manufactured state, would be to re-visit the underpinnings of "civilized" life.

In WW II, women took over men's work in factories, doing a better job for less pay. But after the boys came home, the girls dutifully shipped back to their kitchens, and, instead of exploding with anger, exploded with babies.

Throughout history, women have been be-witching men, beguiling them with their wiles and wares. Men have always succeeded in neutralizing their strengths, today casting them as either over-sexed (horror or "ho") or under-sexed (frigid). Women can never quite get it "right." When women did get it right, men changed the definition of "right," and gave women a new body image, putting them on a diet to take off all those confident pounds they'd gained. Then came the knife.

In the end, it's all about sexuality. And it's women's sexuality that has caused concern for men from Augustus to Augustine to Freud, because of the "lie" men labor under. Men have gone to great lengths to explain their shortened expectations, to defend themselves against any possible involvement in women's sexual "problems."

In this topsy-turvy, upside-down world of men vs. women, sexual pleasure gets mixed up and conflated with sexual violence, rape, sado-masochism, hard core porn, adultery, child sex and prostitution. It becomes tainted, suspect. Women, the source of pleasure for men, are once again blamed. If they dress provocatively, as we like them to do, they are asking for harassment and/or rape.

The fight over abortion during the 20th century is illustrative of this continuing battle between men and women. The issue isn't the killing of life or when life begins. It's women's sexuality; it's whether women control their own bodies. Men, threatened by women's recent ability to be independent of them (not under the control of the "master"), have ratcheted up their attempts to rein them in, to again take control.

Men's control is as necessary for their own interior, personal security—bound up as it is with the lie--as it is for their exterior security: their economic and political domain. Unfortunately, the two are inextricably linked in the continuing befuddlement of men's minds. They still believe in the tooth fairy of "civilization."

QUIZ #5

1. It was considered unhealthy for a woman to:
    a. walk more than five steps before fainting
    b. eat anything denser than puffed air
    c. have anything but a pale, sickly complexion

2. Extra-marital sex (for men) was common during Victorian times because:
    a. the wives were being treated for hysteria
    b. sex was considered too vile for wives
    c. by the time he'd removed all his wife's petticoats, he was exhausted

3. Women suffered from hysteria because:
    a. men have always been reluctant to ask directions
    b. men never like being told what to do
    c. men always think they know what to do

4. In the 1930's women were allowed to:
    a. eat all the food they'd stashed away during the 20's
    b. stop pretending they were flapping ducks
    c. remove the duct tape from their breasts

5. Mr. Kellogg's solution for over-sexed girls was to:
    a. apply a healthy helping of Cornflakes to the afflicted area
    b. make them bathe in a solution of Rice Crispies and honey
    c. force-feed them cornflakes and buttermilk each time they messed up

6. During World War II women were encouraged to:
    a. keep glamour production at pre-war levels
    b. keep their lips extra-red to inspire the red blood of the troops
    c. send pin-ups to the GI's to remind them what the war was about

7. Breasts pose a particular problem for women because:
   a. they're never the right geometric shape
   b. their size fluctuates with the phases of the moon
   c. one of them is always making fun of the other one
   d. being out in front, they're the first thing to be noticed

8. Many people consider rape okay when:
   a. the girl is wearing clothes
   b. the guy gets turned on and might explode, catch on fire or evaporate
   c. the girl is not wearing clothes
   d. the girl has a feminine body

9. Obstetricians were eager to get rid of midwives because:
   a. midwives were better at it and therefore needed more training
   b. they claimed midwives were really witches in disguise
   c. obstetricians kept flunking the midwife exam
   d. most midwives were immigrants and the obstetricians were here first

10. Opponents of abortion argued that:
   a. at two weeks the little kid could already read if the womb were lighted
   b. if the mother snuffed-out her one-day old, who knew what she'd do later
   c. "quickening" was old-fashioned and babies didn't do it anymore

11. The Comstock Law made it illegal to"
   a. send unborn fetuses through the mail
   b. tell your daughter the facts of life in a letter
   c. use baby bottles with un-clothed nipples showing

12. The special "Package Deal" offered to poor women about to deliver was:
    a. a free lobotomy with twins
    b. baby delivered at half-price with other half going toward sterilization
    c. baby put up for adoption without charge if mother wasn't sterilized

13. Men like to make fun of women because:
    a. they are considered sub-human, a funny, separate species
    b. women's bodies lack standard equipment which men find funny
    c. women confuse eating with sex

14. Labor-saving appliances have made it possible for women to:
    a. spend just as much time doing work but with sound effects
    b. wash more clothes in a day than grandma did in a year
    c. fire the servants and shop to content her new hearth, the auto

15. Sexual harassment at work was not a problem until:
    a. women noticed it
    b. men noticed there were women under them clothes
    c. women made unsubstantiated claims that they were human beings

AFTERWORD

"Human Nature" includes both a man and a woman? We've never come close to taking "Human Nature for a spin," to see what "it" could do, to see what we could do, or be. Women have always been an afterthought. We've distorted *Homo sapiens*, trying to do it on the cheap—to make more money (for what?)—"half-assed."

Men, left to themselves, became war-like, took cover, and put women behind them, ostensibly to protect them. The result is a long tragedy, called history.

Women were not thought of as "persons" in the classical world, nor during the Enlightenment, which included the founding of the United States. Today a woman is an almost-person. Women live in a climate that tolerates, if not supports (unwittingly of course), various forms of violence against them: rape, beatings, spouse abuse, incest, and sexual slavery. It's inconceivable that men would tolerate such treatment from other men. And from women? Beyond imagination!

We need to learn to think "outside the box," outside our daily life-as-we-know-it, *everything we currently have and are*. We need to start over, fresh. What we have isn't working. It's brought us and our world to the very brink of self-destruction—doesn't that tell us something? There's no way that women could ever achieve their due within the present paradigm, the way the world's presently "set up," nor should they want to. The present version of "civilization" is a failure, a bust, ready for the trash heap. We tried it, we tried to do it without women—it didn't work. Time to start over. Civilization 2.0.

This time around, we can tell the truth. We've nothing to hide, nothing to be ashamed of, least of all, women. We can go back and reclaim Eden. While there's still time.

BIBLIOGRAPHY

William F. Allman, *The Stone Age Present.* Simon and Schuster, 1994.

Natalie Angier, Women, *An Intimate Geography.* Houghton Mifflin, 1999.

Louis Banner, *American Beauty.* University of Chicago, 1983.

Catherine Blackledge, *The Story of V*, A Natural History of Female Sexuality. Rutgers, 2004.

David Bodanis, *Passionate Minds: The Great Enlightenment Love Affair.* Little, Brown, 2006.

David Bosworth, "Two Sides of a Tortoise: Melville, Dickens and the Eclipse of the West's Moral Imagination." *Georgia Review*, winter, 2004.

Bridenta, Loonz and Strard, (ed.), *Becoming Visible*, Women in European History (2nd ed.). Houghton Mifflin, 1987.

Helen Gurley Brown, *Sex and the Single Girl.* 1962.

Susan Brownmiller, *Against Our Will: Men, Women, and Rape.* Ballantine, 1975.

Joan Brumberg, *Body Project: An Intimate History of American Girls.* Vintage, 1997.

Joan Brumberg, *Fasting Girls*, the History of Anorexia Nervosa. Vintage, 2000.

Nancie Carroway, *Segregated Sisterhood*. University of Tennessee, 1991.

Cesar Chelala, "Changing Cultures to Value Women." *The Philadelphia Inquirer*, April 29, 2007.

Sarah Corbett, article detailing sexual harassment and rape of female soldiers, using Department of Defense data, *New York Times*, Sunday Magazine. March 18, 2007.

Nancy Cott (ed.), *History of Women in the United States*. Oxford.

Ruth Cowan, *More Work for Mother*. Basic Books, 1983.

D'Emilio and Freedman, *A History of Sexuality in America*. Harper and Row, 1988.

Maureen Dowd, *Are Men Necessary*? Putnam, 2005.

Robin Dunbar, *Grooming, Gossip, and the Evolution of Language*. Harvard, 1996.

Barbara Ehrenreich, *Dancing in the Streets*, a History of Collective Joy. Holt, 2006.

Eve Ensler, *Insecure at Last*, Losing it in our Security Obsessed World. Villard, 2006.

Susan Faludi, *Stiffed: the Betrayal of the American Man*. Wm. Morrow, 1999.

Peter Filene, *Him Her Self*, Sex Roles in Modern America. Mentor,1974.

Adrian Forsyth, *A Natural History of Sex: the Ecology and Evolution of Mating Behavior*. Firefly, 2001

Estelle Freedman, *No Turning Back: the History of Feminism and the Future of Women*. Ballantine, 2002.

Betty Friedan, *The Feminine Mystique*. Norton, 1963.

Linda Gordon, *Heroes of Their Own Lives*. Viking, 1988.

Sarah Halprin, *"Look At My Ugly Face!"* Viking, 1995.

Sharlene Hesse-Biber, *Am I Thin Enough Yet*? The Cult of thinness and the Commercialization of Identity. Oxford, 1996.

Helen Lefkowitz Horowitz, *Rereading Sex: Battles Over Sex Knowledge and Suppression in Nineteenth-Century America*. Knoph, 2002.

Terri Judd/Harriet Griffey, "Discrimination against Girls 'Still Deeply Entrenched.'" *The Independent*/UK, May 15, 2007.

Kerber, DeHart (ed.),*Women's America*, 5th ed. Oxford, 2000.

Alice Kessler-Harris, *Out to Work*. Oxford, 2003.

Marie Kopp, *Birth Control in Practice: Analysis of Ten Thousand Case Histories of the Birth Control Clinical Research Bureau*. New York, 1933.

Alex Kuczynski, *Beauty Junkies*. Doubleday, 2006.

Gerda Lerner, *The Creation of Feminist Consciousness*. Oxford, 1993.

Gerda, Lerner, *The Creation of Patriarchy*. Oxford, 1986.

Gerda Lerner, *The Majority Finds Its Past*, Placing Women in History. Oxford, 1979

Krisin Luker, *Dubious Conceptions: the Politics of Teenage Pregnancy*. Harvard, 1997.

Margo Maine and Joe Kelly, *The Body Myth: Adult Women and the Pressure to be Perfect.* Hoboken, 1985.

Rachel Maines, *The Technology of Orgasm.* Johns Hopkins, 1999.

Robert McElvaine, *Eve's Seed,* Biology, the Sexes, and the Course of History. McGraw-Hill, 2001.

Newton, Ryan and Wakowitz (ed.), *Sex and Class in Women's History.* 1983.

Kathy Peiss, *Hope in a Jar.* Holt, 1998.

Roy Porter, *Flesh in the Age of Reason.* Norton, 2003.

Leslie Reagan, *When Abortion was a Crime.* University of California, 1997.

Marjorie Rosen, *Popcorn Venus.* Coward, McCann and Geoghegan, 1973.

Rosalind Rosenberg, *Separate Spheres,* Intellectual Roots of Modern Feminism.Yale, 1982.

Julie Spruill, *Women's Life and Work in the Southern Colonies.* Norton. 1972.

Susan Strasser, *Never Done: a History of American Housework.* Holt, 1982.

Elizebeth Marshall Thomas, *The Old Way,* A Story of the First People. Farrar, Straus, Giroux, 2006.

Colin Tudge, *The Time Before History.* Scribner, 1996.

Marsden Wagner, *Born in the USA: How a Broken Maternity System Must Be Fixed to Put Women First.* University of California, 2006.

Susan Wietzman, *Not to People Like Us*. Basic Books, 2000.

Naomi Wolf, *The Beauty Myth*. Anchor, 1991.

About the Author

It's always bothered me, the way we treat women, the way we're afraid of women, and the general mish-mash of men/women relations, especially when it comes to sex. I'm also aware of my own difficulties in "adjusting," in finding my own definition of "manhood," which began when I was three. I'm still looking.

The "manhood question," that I've sought an answer to, is bound up with how we treat women. And no matter what happens socially or politically, the small gains that women make are soon diluted and all but forgotten. Rape and pillage go on. The Madonna or horror choice for women continues. Our question goes unanswered.

I saw it in Cut Bank, Montana where I grew up, at St. Norbert High school in Wisconsin where I boarded for three of my four years, in the short time (not too short) I was in the army, and at the university—always this "men against women" thing, as if we were competing with them, or angry at them for something.

I'm in my second marriage (twenty-five years). I have grandkids from my first marriage. When I retired from teaching in the Los Angeles Unified School District in 1990, I came upon McElvaine's book, Eve's Seed. He voiced my core argument: women have gotten the shaft from the beginning and men are still shooting themselves in the foot by mistreating them. His book inspired me to put down on paper beliefs that have gnawed at me for years.

I received an M.A. in Catholic Theology from Marquette University, an M.A. in English from the University of Iowa, and I was in the doctoral program of religious studies at the same school for a short time. I've written poetry and I'm working on a novel.

Printed in the United States
97943LV00003B/245/A

9 781434 354402